Following a good Irish education, Finian departed Ireland in 1976 with a Geology BSc Honours degree from Galway University. Accepting a position with Chevron Standard Limited in Calgary, Alberta in 1977, he commenced a 38-year-career in the international oil and gas business. His work across four continents took him to over 80 countries. He currently lives and farms along with his working wife in Hampshire, UK.

In Memory

John J O'Sullivan (1921–2010) and Robin A Wellesley (1928–2020), my father and father-in-law, men who would be kings for the week that we travelled over the Karakoram desert plains along the Turkmenistan Silk Road and rested with the most hospitable of Turkmen in their homes and establishments in the summer of '98. Shown here in the ancient city of Merv.

Finian O'Sullivan

A CRUDE VISION

AUSTIN MACAULEY PUBLISHERS™

LONDON * CAMBRIDGE * NEW YORK * SHARJAH

A CIP catalogue record for this title is available from the British Library.

ISBN 9781398455290 (Paperback)
ISBN 9781398455306 (ePub e-book)

www.austinmacauley.com

First Published 2022
Austin Macauley Publishers Ltd®
1 Canada Square
Canary Wharf
London
E14 5AA

My desire to write this narrative was direct and inversely proportionate to my ability to do so. Reaching pour point after the family summer holiday in 2019, I got underway. The manuscript that evolved thereafter could only be considered intelligible thanks to the dedication and good works of both my wife Diana and my daughter Sophie. Their corrections, criticisms and amendments made the story blossom, for which I am so truly thankful and full of admiration.

Certainly not acknowledged enough but supportive throughout, a huge embrace and show of thanks to Akhtar Sharif for his friendship, encouragement and the early photographs, as he alone travelled with a camera. The core events in the story are joined by the individuals introduced. All these players and the numerous not mentioned played their part in the concert, whether in tune or not, but in such a harmony that most all benefitted from the experience.

I do wish to make special note of two gentlemen in particular, Michael and Simon. For the most part, it felt like they were set on a path of interference, yet they provided the bedrock that launched the narrative. Diana made very clear over the years and at times when my frustration was about to burst, that it was only through these men's early willingness to fund, support and dedicate time to me and my business venture, when naught else would, that Burren Energy could evolve. I shall always be truly thankful for and do acknowledge their role.

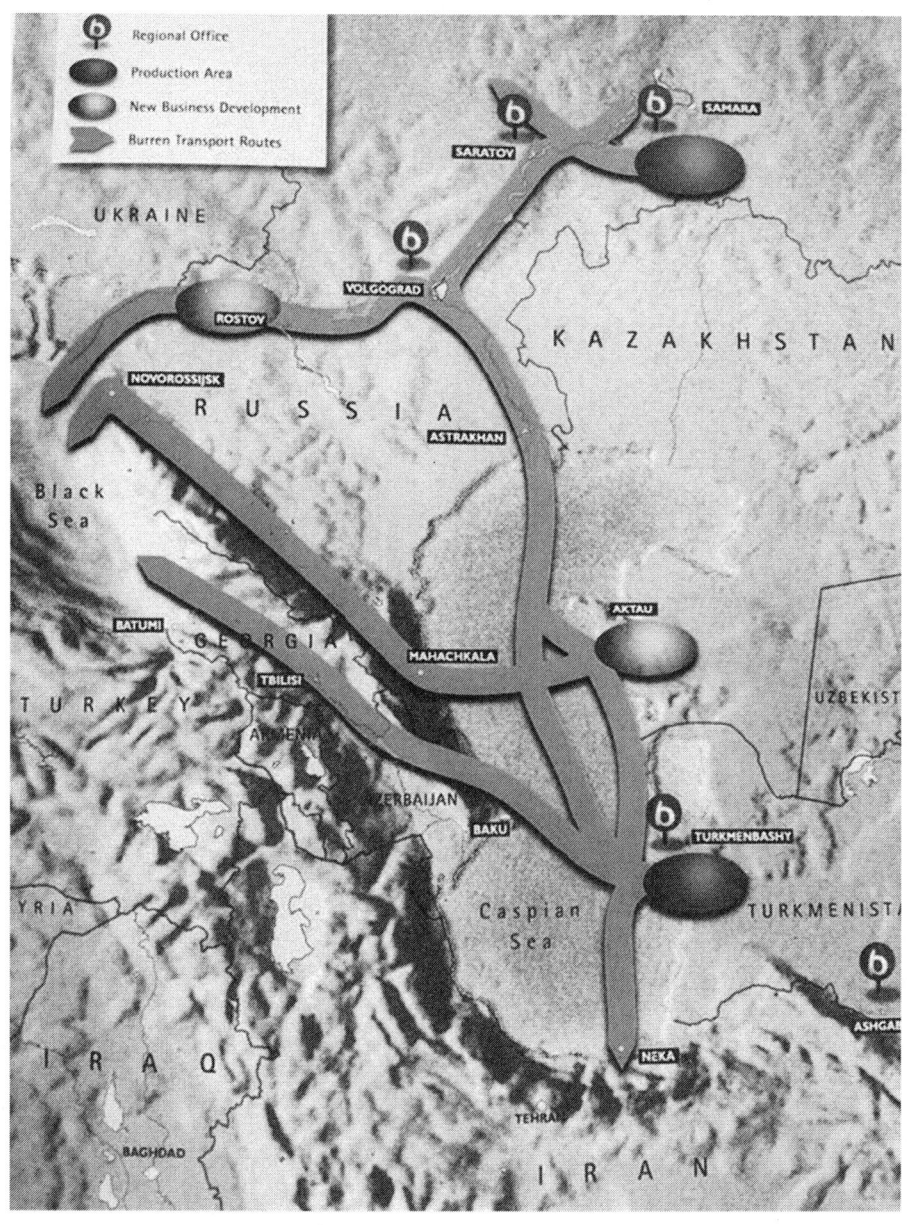

The Game Plan

Timeline of Events

Feb 1993	First visit to Russia and Turkmenistan
Oct 1993	Complete sale of rights to Kotor Tepe Oil
	Field to TYT bank.
Aug 1994	Failed crude oil lift
Oct 1994	Bidding Agreement signed with Monument Oil
Apr 1995	First Successful crude oil lift
May 1995	Incorporation of VSTT
Aug 1996	Burun PSA signed
Feb 1997	Effective date of the Burun PSA
Oct 1997	Incorporation of Burren Energy Plc.
Jan 1998	First Contractor equity crude oil
Feb 1999	Bareboat Charter Agreement signed
Aug 2000	Operatorship and 100% equity of Burun PSA
Aug 2001	M'Boundi No.1 Discovery well.
Dec 2003	Burren Energy Plc listed on the London Stock Exchange
Oct 2007	ENI makes offer to acquire Burren Energy
Feb 2008	ENI completes purchase of Burren Energy

Chapter 1
Setting Out

I was comfortably anxious on arrival at Domodedovo, which was normal for my international travel experience when departing to unknown destinations. Rana paid the driver after I used my only Russian phrase for 'How much', which I estimated I knew in eight languages. Entering the terminal took the edge off the February cold, replaced by the ubiquitous smell of sweat and urine that pervades the public enclosed area of most all socialist countries, in my experience. However, the atmosphere soon changed to a fairytale domain, as the foreigners 'In-tourist' direction took us away from the main flow of traffic into a long corridor which had no roof. Light snowflakes fell festively over the tiled floor making for treacherous walking which Rana found quite impossible, given his city shoes, whilst his black African complexion stood out against the white surroundings. Neither Rana's Russian speaking capabilities, nor my awareness, helped us locate the departure area for our Turkmenia destination as, due to the recent break down of regulations from the Soviet system, it was difficult to decide whether the Central Asian republics were considered foreign or domestic travel. It hardly mattered, as the snow prints of earlier travellers pointed the way to where we quaintly hitched a ride from a passing luggage vehicle, the driver recognising our predicament and, for a small fee, took us to the' In-tourist' departure lounge. I was comforted by the normal levels of confusion and chaos usually associated with socialist policy and purpose as, together, they confirmed that all was going to plan. Sit and wait was the order and we did.

Just after Christmas, my sister Katie's mate, Christian Marner, called. He had spoken with an Anthony Stoddard, just arrived from Dubai, about an extraordinary project involving a car salesman called Mohammad Aziz. This Aziz, whilst on an exploratory business trip to Central Asia, had returned from a capital city, called Ashgabat, where he had been asked as a visiting international business man to tender a written offer for the Kotor Tepe oil and gas field then listed as one of a number of producing fields in their first round of international investment to the hydrocarbon sector. Despite his professed ignorance on the topic, he had discovered, on arrival back in Dubai, that he had won the prized field! He was therefore required to return immediately to commence the necessary due diligence, prior to signing the contract, as it appeared that Aziz had been the only bidder. As neither Aziz nor Anthony knew anything about the exploration and production resources business, Anthony reached out to his old friend, Christian, a gas dealer of note and past business associate, to ask if he knew of anybody capable of assisting. Christian and I had met three years earlier at Katie's house and discussed our mutual, yet distinctly separate, positions and experience in the oil and gas business. My immediate thoughts, given my loosening association with Billy Underwood's Olympic Oil and Gas group in Houston, was that this extraordinary opportunity could be the chance to expand their interests and my own career.

Following a suitable amount of time, in conditions that had improved through the presence of a roof, the call came to embark on a flight to Turkmenia. My knowledge of Turkmenia was limited to its association as part of the Former Soviet Union, but I had reason to trust my travelling companion, a qualified geologist who was attached to the Tanzanian Embassy in Moscow, and this adventure concurred with my belief that true exploration involves travelling into the unknown.

All my hubris was to become a distant dream however when Rana, whilst in the embarkation line, was removed by uniformed immigration police, questioned on his legal certification to travel outside of Moscow and detained. On being led away from the line, his only, and last, words to me were 'blue car'.

Confronting this unique situation, with a blonde airhostess's body language appearing to question my ongoing plans framed by the door entrance, I decided to go with my adrenaline induced travel mood and move into a new chapter. The challenge of not speaking the language, extremely low funds with no local currency, no knowledge of the destination nor the reception expected and the only up to date information being a 'blue car' made me, for the first time in my travelling career, question whether it was wise to embark on the flight. For an instant, I prepared a reputational character saving script and excuse as to why the trip was terminated and aborted. However, the adrenaline, the thrill of the unknown and the knowledge that I had no other options to bring to the business table saw me stride past the blonde and into the most interesting and basic interior that had been my experience to date, bar a Burmese air Fokker flight with a failed door closure cruising at low altitude to Rangoon in '89 or the Dakota cargo flight back to Khartoum in '80.

Buckled into a low-slung comfortable canvas seat beside a native dressed lady and, beneath her, a string bag securing six live chickens made for a moment to reflect on my actions and review the state of play. It was her gold teeth, rich smile and offer of tea in a matching porcelain cup that made me relax and consider the situation more favourably. My mind, as usual when in flight, went into a 'reflective mode'.

****

My caravan in County Mayo, was parked up the track along from the lane that led to Atlantic Drive where would be found the pub and local lads discussing the flood in biblical fashion, with supporting geological talk gathered from the numerous thesis-writing students like me over the years. Stan Reynolds, my university and caravan companion of that summer, would require a life jacket that was part of my diving gear to permit him his weekly bath in the Dolin River. I always used a long rope to tie the jacket and Stan to a tree for safety as the river ran fast, as seen by the suds coming from Stan's long locks. The caravan made for a perfect secluded abode parked beside a dry stonewall but for the morning we were woken by a force 7 earthquake, the epicentre of which was a ram caught between the wall and the caravan, leading to a serious gash. We played out our part as Playboys of the Western World brandishing our geological hammers as Sten guns to frighten any bus or passing tourist from our hillside position. Stan had the motor bike, a Yamaha 125SS, which the old boy in Moycullen would explain was Super Sonic to any passing American tourist buying the pints. Mostly, it worked well for our weekly shopping trips to Louisburg, except for one return journey where we lost our balance, and the eggs, thanks to a dump of sheep manure. Lecanvey just east of the Silurian/Ordovician contact in the region's anticlinorium of Crough Patrick was Mick Mannion and Johnny O'Carroll's lodgings in the shed behind Peggy Staunton's pub. Our meetings were held more often than weekly, when cloud cover was too low for serious field work, at her pub reachable by pedal bike and not that popular given the only seats being uncomfortable pew benches with the local sleeping dogs beneath. Remaining on your bike at the bar was the best course of action.

****

The winter light receding in the west, a guesstimate of air speed and time elapsed supported my calculation and position being approximately 1500 plus miles south of Moscow. Touchdown met the approval of the punters with a handclap of appreciation before disembarkation. Thereafter, the passengers gently walked off the remote airstrip without concern from any authority. I first noted the camels and the arid desert conditions surrounding the tarmac but could not evaluate my position further as the airport was surrounded by low hills silhouetted only by twilight that reached into the darkness. The chill setting in made the senses more aware of the ridiculous circumstances prevailing as I continued to review my situation. How would a chap with my experience get out of this predicament? Moving onwards towards the outer skirt of the apron, I noticed parked cars, the odd blue car amongst them and then, a flash of car lights. Behind the wheel of a battered Lada sat a weathered old Soviet gentleman with his treasured red Lenin collar pin very much on display. Without any conversation we set off into the darkness along a broken sand strewn tarmac road at the healthy top speed of 35kph, with an extraordinary radio accompaniment of 'Hotel California' being squeezed through a meat grinder as the power surged.

The radio melodies in rhyme with the car suspension and the bleak desert horizon relaxed the tension as to where I might be going and set the mind thinking.

****

Undertaking a medical degree would be a struggle for me, I thought, after the surprise of being offered a place to join the medical faculty had worn off that autumn evening in '72. In keeping with family and Irish tradition, I had always nurtured the dream of becoming a doctor. However, my initial offer was for Natural Sciences, which I had accepted. This subsequent offer came as a welcome surprise but led me to reconsider my earlier plans. Wisely, I believe, I faced the options: to please my father and peers with a foregone conclusion to a future known life or to compete within my own capabilities and prepare for an unknown lifestyle. Following a quick trunk call home and a few pints, the desire for the unknown, over the mapped future, brought the matter to a close and my continuation in the science department assured. The totally unexpected arrival of my old headmaster the following week, to query my mental health and questionable drug use following my decision, made it clear that not only was my choice counter cultural but also against the interest of his system. Father Celestine Cullen was a very good man. I felt for his efforts and use of contacts which were apparent in his effort to get my offer. However, the system that Celestine represented was not a system that I honoured or credited with my current position. His was the system that had rejected my leadership qualities and caused division of friendships through falsehood and innuendo, emanating as rumours from my elder brother's bohemian sophisticated lifestyle at Trinity College, Dublin during my last few years of secondary school. However, I had not forgotten that it was Celestine who drove me to the Munster team schoolboy rugby game in Cork, when those responsible refused as I alone was picked which seemed to upset the sport staff. Galway University as a choice was itself an oddity, given the normal graduate flow from Glenstal was to Universities in Dublin or Cork. Yet for me, it was an inspirational choice as it brought the independence of my caravan parked outside the back gate of the college along the right bank of the Corrib River, and peace. Mrs O'Halarahan charged thirty shillings a week for a spot amongst the carpentry sheds debris along with four other student itinerant dwellings. There was no heating, running water or electricity but luckily college facilities were available and conveniently found below the Geology department. Only on a few days over winter would the door require a kick to emerge into a frosty morning, otherwise it was solitude and peace with the token LPs – Madman across the Water, Day at the Races, Night at the Opera and Buddy Miles amongst a few others driven by the battery powered turntable.

With no refrigeration or cooking skill, most all food, except the Sunday night fry from my girlfriend, Annette Carr, was taken at the student restaurant, which could be problematic when a student strike would boycott and force me to break rank for my meal. This would surprisingly prove beneficial as the management would then reduce my meal cost in compensation while the striking students went home to their mum's cooking. One Sunday evening in early January '76, just before my 21st birthday, a mighty storm blew up while I walked back to Distillery Road from Annette's home in Bushy Park. I reached the caravan site with the slates from the neighbouring houses whistling around my head. I found the whole site in chaos including the demolished carpentry shed strewn over my caravan that had remained upright, possibly protected by the corrugated sheets. The

15

caravan to my left, aligned more square to the wind had a 'cheese' cut bisecting its centre from the constant rolling on the stabilising wire. I entered my caravan but could not sleep as she rocked like the old Mail boat in a rough channel crossing. I moved on to find shelter at a friend's home while the slates continued to whistle around.

****

My drive through the unknown, with my Soviet driver in silent mode, took most of three hours. We entered a town along a dimly lit street punctuated by a wonderful carved statue of a laden camel protecting the walking driver from an eroding sand storm. I felt we had reached our destination as the car came to a stop outside a dark authoritarian single-storey building where a suited gentleman stood with an expression of searching bewilderment.

My introductory meeting with Rejab Arazov, the chief geologist for the Balkanabad region of Turkmenistan, could not have been more peaceful as we tried to communicate through gestures. Neither party could speak a word of each other's language yet, through the simple but expressive form of body language, we understood each other enough for the niceties and necessities required. I was extremely content to sleep in the reception complex, without conveniences, and we would meet the next morning in the same place where no doubt the same theatre would continue. I slept a winter's desert sleep as a member of Marco Polo's caravan team would, as they too would have heard the silence broken only by the distant barks of protecting hounds.

Breakfast was a simple affair of home-grown produce that benefited from the natural manure and personal care of the local domestic arid lifestyle. Our roscian games continued until our space was invaded by the chatter of children walking together on the dirt path to school just outside the broken window. Collective wisdom energised both Arazov and I to move and follow the children, which brought us eventually to the local English teacher and her willingness to be our interpreter. It is interesting to reflect back that from this moment the destiny of each was set: Arazov became the fourth minister of Energy of Turkmenistan; the teacher, an international relations manager for the Argentinian oil company with operations in Turkmenistan – Bridas — and I went on to create Burren Energy.

There followed over the next week a program of touring the production facilities, gathering valuable technical data with meetings joined by key management and engineering personal of Turkmeneft, that provided volumes of sensitive information emanating from their database. This burgeoning collection of data would allow me to formulate, with great assistance from my associated Olympic Oil & Gas team back in Houston, a detailed and comprehensive understanding of the past and future potential of this, the largest producing oil and gas field in the western region of Turkmenistan – the Kotor Tepe field. This oil field had over 1000 wells producing in excess of 117,000 bopd, with many hidden or lost beneath sand drifts and dunes. This field, discovered in 1943, had been the main source of crude oil and refined products for the Soviet Empire from the mid-1940s until the development of their vast Siberian resources in the 1970s. The Caspian coastline had been of prospective interest since the late 19th century when the wonderful independent entrepreneurial work of the Nobel brothers and others had opened the region up. They introduced a fleet of vessels that transported the only commercial refined product at that time, kerosene, in barges north through the Caspian Sea into the Volga River system for eventual distribution to western Europe as lighting fuel and the electric power source for its cities.

My lack of corporate style and independent attitude seemed to complement the rather cautious nature of the Turkmen. I rationalised that synergy was achieved chiefly through the age-old technique of social drinking both on and off the job. Each morning's technical meeting with Guildev, the principle petroleum engineer, was accompanied with slabs of local black caviar on hard rye bread followed by copious tumblers of vodka. My level of professionalism required perseverance, patience and stamina. I felt that patience could be afforded, as the majors sought greater materiality in the neighbouring proven petroleum provinces of Azerbaijan and Kazakhstan. The western Turkmenistan diminutive state was further blighted by the industry's perception that it was land locked, without reliable access to western markets, discouraging investment and thereby hopefully providing me broader scope and time to develop the project within my limitations.

I had neither the personal capital investment required nor knew whether Olympic's appetite would stretch to this kingdom despite the geographic, technical and environmental similarities to their home-based operations in both Texas and New Mexico. I believed that Billy Underwood, a man in his early forties, an archetype, paradigm and maverick example of the perfect southern states of the USA oil man who, unlike his modern Wall Street counter parts, had seen crude oil and would consider this project fairly. The departing message that I wanted to leave with these most pleasant hospitable and engaging people, through our translating teacher, was my willingness to convert the commercial potential and political circumstances prevailing into a viable and valuable opportunity for an experienced western oil concern. I had then taken the most difficult step in any new western business project development plan — to go and touch the local earth. It was extremely clear and profoundly evident to a western technical observer that the country, like the region as a whole, had been ravished, exploited and environmentally abused by past masters as its value became diminished and then eclipsed by the prolific Siberian resources and Slavic operators. That historic observation and reality however did not conclude, in my view, that the commercial potential was at an end. On the contrary, the vast amount of investment and infrastructure sunk over the years, unsightly as it was, was still usable if not beneficial to support new investment following a western operating style and technology. This would soon become the rallying call on Wall Street and London markets over the coming decade to gather entrepreneurial investment in the region of Central Asia as a whole. Notwithstanding my realism, there remained the smouldering concern that began to smoke in my embryonic business plan: the lack of control on the limited available shipping. This control factor would become my Gordian cut to open the door to the casino.

Resting in a Tupolev 145, operated by Turkmen Air, we departed the anonymous entry location identified as the main Turkmen Caspian port of Krasnovosk, headed for Moscow and home. On route to Moscow, I contemplated the adventure of the past weeks in this hidden and forgotten corner of the Former Soviet Union. A country the area of France with four million people led by their last politburo leader, Saparmurat Niyazov, who declared independence and a new Republic on the 21st October 1991. A country and opportunity that would be interesting to the initiated, but did the initiated include a car salesman from Dubai?

****

18

This thought led me returning to the hiatus in my career since leaving Australia nineteen months earlier in June 1991 and further back in my past…travelling with my eldest brother John and wife, Geraldine, on that Air Canada flight to another town that I had never heard of until the Calgary flight was called in Heathrow. I went along to make up a balanced foursome with their Calgary based mate, Bolton Agnew, a long-time family friend and resident long haul truck driver despite being a qualified solicitor. Opening the inflight brochure, I noticed the qualifying description for Calgary as being the centre of the west Canadian oil business. This struck an accord with my Galway University Geology degree status which, despite no mention of petroleum geology, provided a sound hard rock geological training and knowledge which could be relevant I thought. A few days later, being hosted at the house of my father's old family friend in Edmonton, Sean Frayn kindly offered to call a friend in the industry and enquire if a line into a job interview could be arranged.

Seated, the next day, in the Calgary office of Dave, senior recruitment officer for Chevron Standard, "What's the name?" he asked.

"Finian Rory O'Sullivan," I replied with a decent amount of Irish lilt. I felt in tune with his response pattern and wavelength.

"Gad!" he said! "I don't think we've got one of those." Our brother, Adrian, collected us from Heathrow bearing a recently delivered Chevron addressed envelope containing an offer for the post of a Geophysicist. I was quick to take mental note of the spelling and the work detailed, as it confirmed for me that there was a smart side to being a geologist. Four months later with my school trunk shipped and the family left for New Year's in Ireland, I put on my new suit and good shoes, gathered my total funds C$82.00 and $1.00 (a career gift from Paddy Gaughan, Geraldine's father, which literally became my last dollar spent some years later while scouting in Somalia) and walked to the Loughton tube station and onto Heathrow. I held a wonderful naivety that waiting at the arrivals hall in Calgary would be the Chevron President and daughter to greet and immediately escort me to a New Year's party…

****

My first Guinness of many to come over the years at the departure lounge bar in Moscow's Sheremetyevo, was taken more for the symbolism than thirst on my accomplishment and achievement in reaching this departure point.

Always on returning trips, whether reaching European airspace from an African nation or reaching the hard track from the Australian outback, there was a sense of relaxation. I felt that recurring sense as I walked toward the BA flight heading for London. I took the levelling experience of the Woking bus and ongoing flyer to Shawford station, walked up the hill to the family home without their expectation of my return and entered to enjoy the family scene.

Gas venting from a site in the Kotor Tepe Field
alongside a derelict Soviet era rig

Chapter 2
The First Failure

I had first heard the name, Billy Underwood, over a good lunch with Tony Treadgold in the River Room restaurant of the Perth Sheraton in West Australia. Tony, a Richard Gere lookalike, had been the rising corporate finance star with First Boston Finance based in Perth when I arrived as the Australian Country manager in February 1982 for Geosystems PTY Limited, a wholly owned subsidiary of Geophsicalsystems Corporation. I was extremely grateful to Tony, for his assistance then to secure a corporate loan for $6m to acquire the second set of Vibroseis™ equipment and put the seismic acquisition crew to work and fulfil our second contract. A difficulty arose however, when the parent company went into bankruptcy, or Chapter 11, in March 1983 leaving my operation responsible and sole guarantor for that and other related debt. (I did manage to pay all Geosystems Pty Ltd corporate debt back in full with interest on term plus three months delay in May 1987.)

At the lunch that day in 1990, Tony asked when on my next trip to the US and in particular Texas, if I could make a cold call to this lad Billy Underwood and in doing so attribute the contact to Tony to benefit and justify his corporate network. A month or two later and without expectations other than the prospect of a lonely weekend in Midland Texas, I did make the call and took up the invitation to stay the weekend in Roswell, New Mexico. I immediately left my motel lodging for a fun-filled weekend with his directors and their wives.

Meeting Billy was akin to smashing down the honoured portrait of the founding father and meeting one's own real John Paul Getty character in the flesh. He was a credited oil finder, the founder of Olympic Oil & Gas Corporation with his valuation of $85 million, the man with 24-hour cash flow including Christmas day accumulating as the digits on a petrol bowser do, rising with the flow. He represented the very image of the successful, independent, hospitable and charming southern state oilman, a character that all young oil boys and girls spend all our careers mimicking and dreaming but never achieving. He stood as testament to my thirteen years in the industry to have been institutional in comparison to what Billy radiated – Freedom. Our relationship, founded over that weekend drinking session and colourful exposition of our respective experiences in his local and my international oil patches, blossomed over the following 12 months. Diana and I hosted Billy and his two founding partners in Perth later that year. I took the opportunity to present exploration opportunities in West Australia and further as my personal travel experience and knowledge went over from the past ten years since leaving Canada. His desire to build from his continental US business into an international asset base company became the fertile ground from where my personal and his business interest merged into a mutual cooperation pack, with Billy as my catalyst and induction to move the family away from Australia and, for me, a departure from the oil service business back to working in the international exploration and project development sector for Olympic Oil and Gas, based in the UK. A career move that, I hoped, would benefit a Billy style operation, given my international experience together with my Chevron/United/Geosystems technical and streetwise oil service experience. From July 1991 through to May 1993, Billy, his team and I made numerous business ventures away from their domestic USA heartland into Peru, China, Venezuela and hopefully, into Central Asia.

Our family move to the UK in July 1991 brought us to Shawford near Winchester from where Diana could reconnect with her Southampton University links and continue her medical genetics work which had itself reached a hiatus in West Australia and would benefit from the move. Our blighted house close to the M3 motorway had a retired coach house building that doubled as my office laid out sparsely with an army surplus wooden trestle table, a second hand office chair and a phone with its own number, all on a hard earth floor but sadly no heating.

That March '93 on arrival back from Turkmenistan saw me sitting in my coat and gloves with the added warmth of my dog on my lap to collate the trip information into a presentable format as best as I could, without computer or photo copier assistance, before packing up and heading for Houston. Once there in the Olympic Oil & Gas 22nd floor office of the Shell Building in down town Houston, Eddie Rodrigues and Byron Bacsmmidt, a two-man petroleum team recognised by their peers and competitors as the best oil and gas finders in their neighbourhood, sat speechless and listened to my story. I presented the data from the recent Turkmen trip that was collated in a format that made them grab it as if this was just up the road in East Texas. I needed to impress upon Billy the unique style and operating experience this new world would bring to his image as the bright new international player. A new world oilman image to afford him numerous applauds from maître d's in his social circle and, in particular, when entering the oil club or Maxim's restaurant in the Galleria and his favourite place to show off his wife, Margaret.

By mid-March, the boys had put together a comprehensive engineering, technical and quantitative summary of the Kotor Tepe field which highlighted the complex nature of the field. I had composed an accompanying introduction outlining the geopolitical status and commercial potential, to broaden their technical report that illuminated both the strengths and the weaknesses of the region without overt reference to the export issue. I was quietly confident that the presentation, in the hands of a hungry independent oil executive, would generate an enthusiastic and positive response and desire to move forward to engage with the authorities. Over the eighteen months that I had worked alongside Billy, I had become aware that Billy's international appetite for foreign risk was not as well developed as he had first believed. With each new project, he became less confrontational and more needful of collaboration and assistance, especially on the issue of finance. To assist him in identifying potential financial source or partner, Billy had latched onto a Mr Roger Tamraz, a silken suited Lebanese businessman with an interesting and inflated past.

Roger Tamraz was a past-his-prime high net worth individual and international network player that had (allegedly) seen him run for the post of President of Lebanon whilst leader of a Christian Democratic political party. His action in such a divided country eventually led to his kidnap and an eight-month term in captivity as a hostage. Roger also claimed to be the founder of Tamoil, a Middle Eastern or Libyan retail outlet. Regardless of that past, he was particularly close to Japanese trading commodity houses interested in investing, as passive non-operating partners, in the international upstream hydrocarbon sector. On one particular trip with Roger to Taiwan, China and Japan over the previous autumn, I sat in the back of the saloon car while in Tokyo listening to Roger and a Japanese industrialist having a conversation climaxing on the future needs of the emergent Chinese nation. In particular, they discussed the steel requirement for an arterial eco-political gas pipeline to span the width of China to achieve any number of geopolitical goals. They believed Central Asia to be the source of the vast quantities of gas required and transported through this trunk pipeline, and the numerous branch lines, to support an industrial heartland for the western desert provinces of China.

They discussed the political, economic and culturally sensitive need for this massive steel manufacturing and logistical project. Their premise was that the principle objective of this political strategy by the Chinese authorities would permit a managed mass migration of Han Chinese to the west for employment and eventual ethnic dilution of the endemic Islamic communities. Employment would be provided and founded on the provision of energy, sourced from Central Asia and delivered through a pipeline constructed primarily from Japanese sourced steel. The project's magnitude was such that the pair realised the steel requirements were not possible through Japanese sources alone. For me, it was the first time that I had heard of the Central Asian region mentioned in the context of an energy supplier or an exporting centre which illuminated a number of points, the most interesting to me being the resultant change of direction of energy flow brought about by the fall of the Soviet Union.

Following my recent trip to Houston to prepare the technical presentation with Eddie and Byron, I suspected that my departure from the Olympic office could be my last as it was clear to me that Billy's international investment comfort zone was firmly directed towards proximal South American ventures and, in common with many of his peer group, permitted the numerous Houston based Spanish speaking exploration teams to prosper. My position in my permanent London base was an obvious outlier to their cost and geographic needs. The opportunity, therefore, to present the Turkmen project as a logical opportunity for a joint enterprise for both Olympic and the Dubai party became my primary mission, in fact, my only mission, as this project was my sole and remaining source of potential benefit.

Dubai in early '93 was a solitary airport supporting the local Creek business community settled in a group of modest high-rise buildings hosting the few international restaurants and apartments. Anthony had one of the more pleasant fourth floor units overlooking the elementary playboy boat marina and jetty. I introduced myself to Anthony and Aziz. The former was exactly the face, style and presence of a well-educated worldly lawyer while Aziz was the classic dish-dash dressed desert car salesman just returned from Friday prayer. I took the first proverb from Mao's Little Red book, where he advocates never to go back on your first impressions and concluded immediately that this pair could not operate the Kotor Tepe oil and gas field. I took them through, in a basic business fashion, the engineering and production facilities, its history and a future program that could be presented to establish commercial viability for the contract and the field. They were, of course, immediately taken by the proven producing and probable petroleum figures that supported the size and magnitude of the field. I then asked the five-million-dollar question: had Aziz got the $5m signature bonus? The amount required to satisfy the bidding agreement with the Turkmen authorities and commence financing field operations. His reaction was immediate and very Arabesque with the wide-open eyed look and silence. I could gauge that Aziz had become transfixed by the amount of zeros that had been attached to my computation and any resulting scenario for the value of the project. However, by bringing the conversation down to earth with the bonus payment as the key point of order, it was clear to me that Aziz was not in a position to fulfil this basic requirement. I had yet to mention the contractual requirement to guarantee, corporate or otherwise, a commitment to a further $50m new capital investment plan over the first five years of the 25-year project agreement. There was an obvious lack of knowledge, experience and the international financial acumen required to undertake the ownership and operatorship of a project of this nature.

In conclusion, I made it clear to the pair that to satisfy the political, technical and financial requirements within the international oil and gas industry for a project of this size and nature, the host government would require that an experienced operator underwrite the liability for all operating activities, both above and below the surface, including and not limited to environmental, employee and third-party damages through, initially, a corporate guarantee. And further, in my view I added, the Turkmenistan government would require that Operator to have a good understanding of the politics in the region and the ability to manage the politics. On this last point, I thought, a tribute could be afforded to Aziz. Throughout my presentation, I did place emphasis on the lack of an export option. As a corporate lawyer, most all my points made sense to Anthony but for Aziz, this was a tonic. He could see his carpet rise amongst his community and beyond. The response did have one immediate result which gave me solace: an Olympic Oil & Gas partner or equivalent, along with my international experience, was very much in demand.

To agree a semblance of participation between the parties I proposed and agreed terms of engagement on a dedicated monthly 'consultant' basis at my Olympic monthly cost plus 5%. This would quieten and distance the Houston hounds while giving them access to project development and allow me to build my own relationship and participation in a project which, if successful, could be a career's work. That we agreed and finalised an agreement should have been a red flag to me, as I had earlier surmised that Aziz, the car salesman and Anthony, the in-house corporate lawyer, had scant authority or financial support to enter into a binding agreement with Olympic. However, the document was signed and faxed through to the Houston office from where it would look perfect to Billy and Olympic as the agreement covered their financial exposure for me with the benefit of the small financial uplift and potential participation in the project. This would not prove to be the case as, within three months, all bets were off and I would be left with a large credit card airfare expense and no income.

From that initial meeting in late March with Anthony and Aziz in Dubai, the following six-month period proved most stimulating for me as we travelled and communicated on a weekly if not daily basis. The collaborative style and work experience highlighted my isolationist manner and business style that had been governed from my solitary management experiences in the oil field service sector since leaving Chevron twelve years earlier. I relished the company of non-oil industry personalities, listening to their career experiences and idiosyncrasies, which seemed extremely mild in comparison to my own. My technical commentary and contribution whilst limited to the upstream (collectively hydrocarbon exploration, development and production) sector only, and then, to geophysical acquisition and processing techniques and amusing stories, mostly credible and supporting to their basic levels of the oil industry. I realised that over the past years I had not generated nor had wished a collection of individual friends from within the business community, as they seemed to part as quickly as we found each other, through retrenchment at the next cash or, if a client, the next contract drama. The pair gave me support and a sense of security with their legal and ethnic regional business knowledge, which merged us into a 'three amigos' and a presentable, simple yet formidable front for the objective at hand. Within the three, I knew my place as a consultant rather than an equity player, which did not reduce my commitment and I was always prepared, as I kept my passport at hand, to respond to their call. On one occasion, I left a Sunday lunch invitation in Winchester and travelled directly to join Aziz in Istanbul. I then proceeded to travel for the next week in Central Asia in my Sunday best plus an acquired pair of swimming trunks, a new shirt plus acquired toiletries, all carried in a sturdy PINKS (tm) plastic bag.

Anthony had a very proper Eton Oxbridge background, completed with city and international exposure that presented well. I was personally delighted to find that he had the wonderful refinements that come with such a beneficial education, equality and universal respect without any of that class-ridden fault of pretension or conceit. He would maintain his position in both casual and business meetings as the quiet, conscientious calculating one with the intelligent turn of phrase that could rescue or amuse a difficult situation. He surprised me by not wishing to lead the discussion but rather provide ubiquitous intellectual fighter cover. When alone, without Aziz, we enjoyed games of chance for small change or abstract betting counters. Over a three-day stay in a Moscow monastic house then converted as a guesthouse when all business had ceased due to the Baring Bank collapse fiasco, we adopted a game of RISK conformed to the map that we carried of the oil fields of Western Turkmenistan and gambled over ownership of the individual wells. He would never raise his temper or his voice despite the opposing view or business obstacle, which was most reassuring and educational.

Aziz on the other hand could be difficult, obstinate and unpleasant with individuals that he deemed insignificant for the purpose at hand. A characteristic failure in many but more prominent in Arab dealings as was my experience. Yet, and with the exception of Sharif, he was the most devout religious man I had the pleasure to travel alongside. His moments for salat proved most problematic on occasion when travelling by plane, as prayer en route was not acceptable to the Faithful. On one occasion, we held up the departure of a Turkish Air flight while he prayed and I stood guard at the foot of the airplane steps on the tarmac of Ataturk airport. On another, his total lack of direction and subsequent animations became a wonderful sight and source of amusement to me and others when he realised that the duration of the flight exceeded the limitation for his salat and therefore committed him to prayer on the plane, but in which direction? I had to come to his assistance despite being seated four rows behind in giving him the approximate direction of the qibla. Without a doubt, this diminutive, medium-sized egg-headed, slightly overweight car salesman from Dubai could be fun, but as is their custom with foreigners, rarely would be.

The stage was set for the poor man's Aladdin court in a far-off arid desert country where a star would lead the ego and his political minion toward the pot of gold. The first course of action was the immediate requirement for Aziz, Anthony and I to make an unsolicited visit to the energy minister in the capital town of Ashgabat. As would soon become normal, we took the first available Turkmen flight out of Dubai, which happened to be a charter flight, near full with domestic white goods excess baggage cargo accompanying the owners, the new Turkmen middle class, the new class of wealth that had appeared overnight with Independence and release from the Soviet regime, after a weeklong 'shop till you drop' tour. The only meeting time available with the minister, at such short notice, was 05.45 and we duly attended. It was obvious that the Islamic preference or code meant all to the Turkmen minister, Mr Oshanov. With cultural and religious etiquette exchanged, he was certainly under the impression and belief that he was dealing with a reliable and competent investor and one that, having presented his technical 'western team', was duly afforded the credit and the open door to commence discussions with the contracts team at Turkmeneft, the state regional operating concern for the Balkanabad region. I was delighted to get this green light as it brought me back to my contacts, Mr Arazov and Guildev. With what seemed to me to be a hastily assembled group of local contacts and a middle-aged lady, Latiffa, as the translator, the team went to work.

In parallel and with more assiduity, two additional international companies had advanced negotiations on offshore producing blocks with the Turkmen ministry and, shortly after our commencement, would sign 25-year contracts. The contract terms of engagement and associated boilerplate clauses were the same for all three contracts (both onshore and offshore) under discussion, except for the respective work program proposed within the initial five year period. The contract terms proposed in each contract had an equity ratio for the government and investor 51%:49% fiscal arrangement, with the investor providing all the funds through to payback. There was an obvious and insurmountable downside to the terms proposed by their failure to include clear definitions and process to accounting, fiscal or legal international standards or, in the event of a dispute or default, a process of arbitration or force majeure.

All of which, in my view, was collectively an invitation to a court appearance and a good cause to delay signature until rectified.

The two international companies, Bridas, an Argentinian fishing company owned and directed by the Bergulrone family and Larmag, a Dutch registered company owned solely by the real estate magnate Lars Magnusson, had both blazed a trail to an agreement without addressing numerous issues and, in particular, my concerns. Both had a different agenda as becoming of the two distinctive charismatic personalities, yet both lacked international oil contract experience as neither had performed under contract elsewhere or, in the case of Larmag, even operated before in the oil business. Both individuals had well-publicised history from their respective countries of origin which detailed past financial dealings illuminated with large foreign capital tax credits, currency gains from interesting domestic or foreign deals. The suggestion that their respective investment model was a form of money laundering was both suspicious and instructive to an early player in Turkmenistan.

My concern of my party's financial liquidity and reduced circumstances notwithstanding, and hoping that time would be the delaying tactic to bring some resolution, I continued to fully engage in the proposition of a technical program inclusive of capital and operation expenditure for each of the first three of the initial five-year plan. I wanted to focus on cash generation in the early years to enhance oil production and an exploration budget, inclusive of a seismic program, to identify the first deep exploration well in the fourth year. With two wells thereafter, that would collectively satisfy the $50m contractual expenditure commitment. All expenditure henceforth, up to and over the term of the 25-year contract, would be discretionary. The contractual disputes that later caused fractious litigation and belligerent relations between Larmag, Bridas and the government would centre on the lack of legal and accounting definition as to whether the foreign investor's $50m was new capital, dedicated to finding new oil, or $50m cumulative capital expenditure acquired from both new cash flow, derived from finding new oil, and the cash attributed (to the Turkmen account) from existing oil. Sadly for the Turkmen, their legal advice fell short of this clear understanding or definition.

Over numerous trips back and forth with Anthony and Aziz presenting and negotiating our fiscal business model, I had built up a good working relationship with Arazov and Guildev both of whom by then held senior management positions in the regional office and would hold ministerial or other political positions in the future. I was making every effort to encourage them to add new drafting into the contract that would address my concerns but was met with strong resistance, particularly from the ministry member, Essanov, who I felt was being enforced by a higher authority. I did, however, feel that I was getting the regional managers to understand and note my concerns to be in their current and future interest. Our meetings went into a holding pattern while Aziz and Anthony made legal representations to the minister. It was in essence all a stalling tactic for time while a source of funding, in particular the signature bonus amount of $5 million, became available, yet there was also a political and commercial factor in not wanting to be vilified when the ministry realised the limitations of their proposed contract terms.

By late April, I was back in London circulating amongst my few industry acquaintances. It became a pleasure and a benefit to enjoy frequent use of Christian's Saville Row offices which usually included a good lunch at Cecconi and a game of balut. I could not afford to play the big stakes game as my funds were extremely tight and hoped my own reduced circumstances were not that obvious in their company. It was during this period that I re-introduced myself to Brian Thurley, a member of the real oil and gas London community and senior geologist at the London based and listed company Monument Oil. I had first met and presented to Brian in the Nymex London office when his company held a non-operating working interest in Thailand acreage. It was through my Australian seismic acquisition work bidding on this block for a large seismic contract that brought me the introduction. Brian had shown then not just his good technical appreciation but also an entrepreneurial spirit and ancillary style which I wanted to cultivate and get 'friendly' advice.

I continued to tempt Billy with constant updates of developments on the Turkmen opportunity, which met a constant retort as to why there was a failure of Anthony to pay my consulting fee which was then moving into a third month, but soon the message came that Roger Tamraz wished to meet in Istanbul. The meeting was proposed as an introductory discussion with Aziz and Anthony, a proposition that would include an introduction with a Turkish interested party, should Roger see the fit. I was delighted with this development and began to get the excitement of the chase and prepared for the trip.

Well cushioned into the Ciragan Palace Kempinski Hotel in Istanbul and enjoying a lobby coffee, I experienced a most arresting view through the open balcony to the distant bush. The vista broken by the red hull of a passing oil tanker, only metres away, navigating its way through the tight stretch of the Bosphorus. This truly remarkable view would be matched, a few years later, following our own chartered and operated tanker passing through the same straights. It was a wonderful omen. For the first time, I thought that I could see some blue sky.

The meeting between Aziz, Anthony and I with Roger accompanied by three directors of the TYT Bank started extremely well, with an introductory chat that led into a detailed technical presentation followed by an exchange of views and content mostly directed to commercial and political discussion. This agenda continuing over a three-phase meeting schedule that included dinner that evening, a morning session and a concluding afternoon session at their bank headquarters. Throughout, Anthony provided the confident British cover for financial, legal and contract issues whilst I provided, in addition to the technical and fiscal program, the light entertainment with anecdotal memoirs of the Turkmen officials, their characteristics and expectations, which cemented what looked like a good union. However, Aziz started to become uncomfortable as the bankers amongst the group seized on the capital figures. He seemed incapable of accepting the magnitude and returns the project would bring if properly financed and operated. The arrangement and offer from TYT to participate in the project together with Aziz holding a 'Mr 5%' carried interest was presented right there to him. Regretfully, his intransigence won that day as Anthony felt that he could not overrule what he saw as a partnership of equals, with Aziz being the 'Turkmen contact man' and therefore of great importance. I thought otherwise, but as Aziz had managed to insult our Turkish friends with his Arabic offhand manner, their offer to enter into a partnership was withdrawn. However, it was not to be the end of the Roger/TYT Bank interest in Turkmenistan, as it became abundantly clear over the next few days that the Turkish government influence in the region, that was being promoted by Saudi funding, was not limited to a few oil fields but included the launch of a satellite held in a geostationary orbit of the Central Asian territories to feed Islamic programming and propaganda. This particular episode ended in disaster later that year with the failure of the launch vehicle from a launch site in French Guyana.

It didn't take long for the rogue element from Roger to make its appearance. Sensing correctly that Aziz had neither the signature bonus nor a broad network ability to complete the deal, he directed his team to deal through the Turkish lobby in Ashgabat and pursue his goal. I took quick steps to highlight their lack of technical experience and in doing so convinced Billy that more than at any time, the arrival of a genuine financially credible western oil concern to the party would deliver positive results and, therefore, to make a visit in person to the minister and present the 'real' oil man view. This course of action also had its problems, as Billy could quickly understand the opportunity to support Roger and the Turkish group to reach the end game, but the unknown quantity was the strength of Aziz' relationship with the minister, which was seen to be crucial. At this point, I was prepared to play both sides of the fence, as Billy's Olympic would prevail as the engine for whichever of two options of baggage the Turkmen minister would choose which left me in a saddle that would yield me a future with the project and a beneficial result.

I accompanied Billy on the recently opened Turkish Air flight from Istanbul to Ashgabat, which initially had a settling effect for Billy who was way out of his geographic comfort zone. The drinking soon started and sadly did not stop for the remainder of the three days in country. The whole presentation and relationship building objective was totally lost as meeting after meeting with minister and technical teams was reduced to a slurring flow of hubristic diatribe and, for unknown reasons, presentations of United States Geological Survey legal jargon that was of absolutely no value or importance or called on by the minister. Billy had completely lost the plot, the gig and the country's attention.

Seated together in our appointed Soviet styled accommodation on the third afternoon, I wasn't upset with Billy but was personally in despair as I knew that I had no future with Olympic without the Turkmen project which he had recently lost through a weakness in his personality, and that was most disappointing. The man that had shown me the road to 'Freedom' within the industry had fallen at a simple fence of locality. All he had to do was embrace the project, despite its location, until it was commercially refined through legal contract and sell it on. The trading instinct had failed him. Billy, then in a more sober moment, requested a flight out through London for us both and him to the USA. I took up my poor and only option to remain with the project and so his flight was duly arranged as far as Istanbul. His departure from the scene punctuated not only the termination of formal technical and commercial support, but also my job with Olympic Oil & Gas.

My refusal to leave with Billy severed our relationship although we parted on good terms. Truly on my own for the first time, a sole player without income except what I thought was due from Anthony and Aziz, a state I would remain in without a secure or monthly income for the next 24 months. Whether Billy made the call or not, it did not take Roger and his minions more than 24 hours to make their appointments and presence in Ashgabat felt as they moved in ambassadorial convoy from government building to building. Aziz had real opponents for his Kotor Tepe prize, opponents that could show both the money and a similar flowing Crescent Flag.

What followed within days of our meetings can best be described as a scene from a prime television courtroom drama. In the Turkmen Energy Minister's conference room, the minister and his technical staff separated from the Aziz team, inclusive of me. Across the room was Roger's team, inclusive of their TYT Bank finance men. On this occasion, there was no loyalty shown by the Turkish team other than support for the two-nation status both historic and to the future. Their private national bank credentials unquestioned, they opened with their pitch that included almost all of my technical, commercial and operational text and view, given that they had this from the meetings the previous month in Istanbul. They seemed to be racing into an unassailable position until Aziz rose to make our impassioned speech that only true car salesmen can achieve. With tears in his eyes and noble Islamic demonstrations and expressions, he slowly dragged the room's attention back to his original claim and handshake.

There came the moment when his summations were made, and delivered up to the judge and jury, and silence prevailed. I could see my career cliff edge. I could sense that the Energy advisory team were divided – Arazov and Guildev, my supporters from Balkanabad region, being for Aziz, whilst a quiet and serious man, Essanov, based at the ministry in Ashgabat, was favouring Roger, who held greater political and financial support. Whatever Aziz had on the energy minister, Oshanov, would never be known, but he favoured the argument of Aziz who won that day. It may well have been the minister's misjudgement as he was replaced by Essanov within a month.

Over the hot summer months, the new minister made his position and effectiveness known to the local and extremely small, foreign community. The constant political calls from the Turkish group (Roger and TYT) made the field extremely one-sided, but the fasting season lowered the pressure and gave Aziz the break, as I saw it, to find the money and amend what I took from our first meeting: he had to get the $5 million signatory bonus. What became my modus operandi and objective through meetings both in London, and over the phone to Dubai with Anthony, was to get Aziz to accept that a deal with the Turkish group and Roger, before the Turkmen authorities threw out his claim resulting directly from political Turkish pressure, was essential.

It was then over three months since my departure from Olympic and, more worrisome, neither Anthony nor Aziz had made any payment for my accumulated consultancy bills issued by Olympic or, following their departure, by me. I had paid my credit card travel costs from my diminishing reserves, which again had been claimed but not paid, and knew that it was the beginning of the end game for Aziz and his Islamic belief in the relationship business.

Anthony had gone AWOL which concerned and even panicked me as it was not the first time in my career that I could see the whites of my creditor's eyes. In complete abandonment to my purse or my value, I took a cheap flight to Dubai and talked my way past the office management, who knew me as a friend of Anthony, and into his apartment and took sanctuary. Anthony was neither surprised nor upset to find me staked-out in his apartment as my numerous messages left with his office had caught him up at some point. Rather, he was accepting that Aziz had not got the funds for the signatory bonus and so my long-time advice to bring the deal to a close with the Turkish group was correct and the only option. We agreed that I would make contact with Roger/TYT bank to broker a deal with Aziz, as I knew that the closing date for a second round of tenders and in particular Block 1, a significant offshore development play, was imminent and of interest to the Turkish Bank. I proposed to Roger that, along with the Turkish Bank, he might wish to resolve the first-round bidding jam, through the 100% acquisition of Aziz's claim for a one-off payment of $3m for the rights to negotiate the onshore Kotor Tepe block. Should this option be agreed and adopted by the Turkmen, then it would see his and their credibility and political currency rise beyond all expectations.

Similar to most of all the high moments of the last 10 months, the scene within and outside the new Independent Hotel in Ashgabat on that October day was a mixture of 'High Noon' and 'OK Corral'. While Anthony and I completed the deal particulars and traded documents with Roger and his legal team within, Aziz remained outside holding a small crushed leather bag which he periodically shouted up to the closed window 'had the $5 million signature bonus money in cash and was on his way to the ministry to register the payment'. Aziz remained on the parking tarmac as we all left the hotel with the deal, shaken but not concluded, as it would require the minister to sign the assignment letter and accept the Turkish TYT Bank* bid of $20 million signature bonus for the offshore Block 1 as well as the $5 million for the onshore Kotor Tepe block.

Following the minister's positive reception and back in the Independent Hotel, the Turkish group made over two post-dated cheques for a total of $3 million. One for Aziz and, before completion of the second, I took Anthony aside to request that I receive some payment at this junction. Anthony agreed but Aziz would not contribute. Anthony requested that the Turkish group make out a third cheque for an amount of $46,000.00 which would be deducted from his half only and that it not be post-dated. They did and I had some money.

The following morning, in the lobby, both sides, as is often the case following a momentous deal, took separate sides in easy chairs. Neither party conversed except for me as it was clear that I had played for both sides in reaching the conclusion. While seated close to the Turkish team, I was asked by Roger for my view on their Block 1 tender. I commented that I felt that their bid price was unnecessarily high given the lack of any visible competition. Roger responded that it was correctly high as it protected Turkish national pride and image. In conclusion, and in a throw away manner, he asked what I was going to do in the immediate future as, having brokered this deal (and at least earned a small sum) I was surplus to their requirements. My response was pharaonic in foresight: that I would set out to form a shipping company similar to the business model of the Nobel Brothers of the 19th century that could control exports from foreign operators along the eastern Caspian oil fairway. Control of dedicated tonnage could provide leverage to earn participant interests in upstream projects. Roger went silent as he then realised why and what I had not explained over the period of negotiation.

****

It was the silence rather than the acute cold or darkness that roused me. It was so silent. Lifting my head from under the covers, I felt the cold which was real cold and heard the shifting strides outside on the soft snow and whispered speech, all relayed a problem. In remote location camps, a generator noise is your nanny. Outside the temperature was -64 degrees. The gas tank had frozen and no car moved as the foot mats and tires became too brittle. Our position just south of Lesser Slave Lake in north eastern British Columbia was well known for cold generated by atmospheric reversal, but this was sharp cold. Circumstances greatly improved with the placement of empty pineapple tins filled with diesel-soaked toilet roll set alight under the gas tank. The flow of gas and heat gave relief as we went on to work as the temperature rose above -37 degrees. I trembled as the twin engine Otter accelerated on skids along the access road towards the growing stature of the rig. Holding tighter and concerned as the Chevron pilot parried the engine strengths to compensate for the plane's take off angle and divert the nose away from the rig, I thought of my early days in Calgary with Emmett Urquhart, a fun lad that made me welcome at Chevron over those first days of introduction to office protocol full of practical jokes. In this spirit, I took Emmett for a drink with a blonde and mentioned he should not stare at her facial expressions as she had a false eye. The session became animated and expressive as both became more concerned and conscious of their respective facial confrontations, which amused me no end as she had perfect vision! We created between us a tycoon venture in share dealing: while most of our colleagues paid for the lunch time training course we invested our cash and made drinkable gains. Bolton, with whom I house shared, and I acquired one house and speculated on others as the Calgary real estate market was buoyant over my time there, given the wealth of the town and influx of people to Calgary in the late '70s. The experience of Calgary, together with Chevron, was a brilliant start that gave me a wonderful technical understanding in addition to a discerning business interest in people and cash management.

My two and half years at Chevron and in Calgary had been short but rewarding, both for its practical and academic qualities. Over my time there, Chevron had given me invaluable training through each of its stratigraphic and structural three-week geological field courses, a ten-day period of hell at the Linear Operators computer school in Houston and a position of staff geophysicist that gave me sole use of the extremely advanced computer processing modelling program – Wellmod™. Ahead of its time by 20 years, the program computed vertical and lateral velocity changes (technology that supports the contemporary Hawkeye™ system) with rock density and presented the subsurface anomaly in a chromatic form.

It was my youthful desire to travel which motivated my escape from the insular and institutional existence of Calgary which had followed on from my tertiary education. My decision to go forth to experience the broader international industry was born out of the realisation that I yearned for more genuine, practical experience. I resigned in April '80, worked my termination period, locked up my house and, with a contact arranged, set off to fulfil my hopes of becoming a seismologist on a seismic crew in the commercially active Orinoco river delta of Venezuela. I took Diana's car, as she had returned to the UK and would join me later that year in Los Angeles, and drove to California. My departure and move from the stable white-collar upstream oil industry over the railway tracks to the service oil industry side was counter flow and considered unique if not stupid. It was the hippy aged music that most excited me as I drove south over the border using my Albertan driving license as my national entry card and, heading on Highway 24 through Montana, Idaho, Utah,

Nevada and on to California, terminating at the end of Highway 5 at the Santa Monica pier. Meeting with Pete Gathings, a no frills fifty plus WW2 marine with distinctive small-man syndrome and the Vice President of the Eastern Hemisphere for United Geophysical Corporation, who gave me a job as his assistant based in Pasadena, California was my first taste of the service side of the business. In his terminology, our role was 'the turd in the punch bowl' and why remained to be seen. My objective and wish to get to Venezuela was put on hold, as he requested I attend a week basic financial short course in Los Angeles before heading out from their head office in Pasadena to visit their numerous international field operations that together formed the Eastern Hemisphere division of United Geophysical Corp.

The small plane lifted its nose over a ridge of the Papua New Guinea highland when the pilot commented that 'we're committed to land as there is no room to circle' here; I looked ahead at the approaching cliff or peak towering into the sky. The Porgera base landing strip was a WW2 Japanese temporary strip laid at a 45-degree angle with no room to miss. "In the event of an abort landing, we're compelled to run off between the trees to detach the wings," he said... Harry Morley's face of imperial displeasure at the sight of the local chiefs beating their entourage to get first access to the overcrowded and last schedule daily flight from Enugu to Lagos was a picture only Lady Curzon would admire. "Dignity," he muttered as we lost our seats to the onslaught. Harry embodied the British presence. Tears would roll down his cheeks as they always did on his fourth beer and the retelling of his memory of being a boy in 1947 present for the last Raj sepoy salute in Delhi and the lowering of the flag. Regardless of his colonial strength that day, we were still short a flight to Lagos when there came the roar from within the low clouds, the appearance and approach of a passenger jet—not just any passenger jet but an Aer Lingus 737 with full Irish stewardess and flight crew... From first light, I could see the translucent scorpions clatter along the underneath spar of the A frame tent. I was careful not to jolt the narrow structure as one could easily fall. With the flaps open for ventilation, there was a good view over the Sud wetlands of southern Sudan to the Ethiopian mountains. Breakfast would be the same hardboiled egg and tinned fruit with black coffee. There was never fresh milk for our 'lost' seismic crew, working as it was continuously southward into Chevron's vast Sudanese exploratory land. It was Bob Sparrough, the corporate head accountant, who questioned the order for the body bags at the monthly crew account reconciliation meeting at the head office in Pasadena, California. I explained that on my last visit to the Nigerian delta crew there had been an attempt robbery and a shooting of one of the criminal party. It was my opinion that it would only be a matter of time before a crewmember was shot. He showed no emotion and spoke only to ask to which account he should charge the bags.

We spent our honeymoon in Stalinist social democratic Tanzania, where food and light bulbs were at an onerous premium, as we prepared a tender for a five-year contract proposal with Shell. The itinerary was quite a change for Diana, who had planned our honeymoon trip back to LA via her family in Florida, as the jungle bars and remote hostel we found appeared as a mirage before us as we completed the first scout day out from Dar es Salaam. The lack of planning and impromptu arrangements peaked with the experience of the prison cell in Morogoro. The cell proved the safest place to reside that night with the local tribal troubles the region was experiencing at the time.

The long stare between the elder and I as I sat in the back corner seat crushed by the crowd leaving the debris-strewn town of Hargeisa for my return to Mogadishu laid bare the distinctly different universes that we traversed. I knew that my efforts to bring investment through a new seismic proposal to the region would not clear the basic hurdle, as war was imminent. His consuming stare lasted from the time it took for all the bundles of khat (Catha edulis) to be loaded on top of the bus, right up to our departure that followed the only tarmac road along the continental escarpment before descending on to the coastal plain to the town of Berbera.

****

On the flight home, I considered that my career was moving inexorably away from secure employment. Not for the first time since the family's departure from the picture book lifestyle of Perth and Western Australia in July '91 did that image of the 500-piece jigsaw picture of the family home with paddock, pool and garden, with the three girls happy as the wife builds her career in the West Australian genetics community jolt against the current realisation I was attempting to build a similar picture in the UK, but with a jigsaw of 10,000 pieces. I continued to find weakness with my direction since my professional days with Chevron in Calgary, destined as I may have been for high office as the staff bound professional geophysicist. Instead I had pursued the field geophysicist itinerant life…

*The TYT Bank went into liquidation over the Turkish Lira crisis in May 1994. They failed to execute the Effective Date for the Turkmen Blocks which were later relinquished. Block 1 was years later signed and successfully operated by Petronas. Kotor Tepe remains to this day operated by the Turkmen national oil company. Aziz did not cash his post-dated cheque and to my knowledge remained unrecompensed.

Chapter 3
The Second Failure

Over the winter months and into 1994, I knew I had to reconcile my family financial circumstances and compose my Caspian business model. In addressing the former, I considered my current career as a fair-weather sailor, out beyond the point of rescue from the local coastal community, with any rescue relying on the luck of a passing vessel. The £20,000 odd sum exchanged from the TYT cheque in addition to the modest reserves retained after making a deposit on our house in Shawford would manage the family requirements of mortgage and education for the immediate future. These funds, in addition to Diana's part-time clinical genetics salary from the NHS, would provide for the basics with no structured holidays, new carpets or other distinguishing household effects.

This business model, or 'The Game Plan' as I liked it to be referred to, grew from the previous year's Turkmen knowledge and experience together with my extremely limited shipping knowledge. Together, I merged both with my broader international business operating and logistical experience in remote and diverse locations. My proposition was to derive the optimum theoretical fleet requirement to effect an economic return from a virtual remote location crude export operation, whether that be offshore or onshore production. The local geographic and maritime knowledge that I had collected over the previous year in Turkmenistan was the nugget. In simplistic business terms, there were two foreign investors or producers, Bridas and Larmag, with a potential third – TamrazTYT, all of whom would require and wish to receive hard currency. There was one load port and two jetty locations along the Turkmen Caspian coast line, of which only the jetties would be available as export points to the foreign investor. I knew the distances from both jetty locations to the numerous discharge ports, the average cargo size per vessel (4500 tonnes or 32,400 barrels equivalent) and the approximate load time, but not the discharge time at the available discharge ports. The fundamental problem that prevailed was that the contemporary and conventional trading ports within the Caspian Sea had only a soft currency or barter counter trade value for crude, which had little or no interest to my Game Plan as a western investor would only be interested in a hard currency return. The optimally valued discharge ports on the European Black Sea and prized ports of the Mediterranean offered hard currency in exchange. On the basis of crude exchanged for hard currency, and knowing the vessels had a cruising time average of nine knots which enabled me to estimate the voyage turnaround time per vessel between the jetties and the hard currency trading discharge ports (plus a guesstimate discharge time), I built a matrix utilising the Turkmen logistics. From this matrix, I could estimate both the fleet required to logistically support graduated levels of export production and a relative transportation 'cost' per barrel for a variety of nominated voyage discharge ports from the respective export jetties.

Without a trans-Caspian pipeline, direct access to the European Black Sea ports from those along the eastern Caspian and beyond could only be achieved through the Russian river/sea system, and that demanded, as I had learnt from Arazov, a Russian flagged vessel. The historical and current trading facts that I had also learnt from my conversations and reading indicated that the value of the accrued cargo would increase exponentially the further the transport distance between the load and discharge ports. Simply put: getting the crude oil or product to a western market increased the value per barrel far above the cumulative cost of transportation and production; the value premium was in retaining control of the title of each barrel through the transportation or midstream sector, which in turn would give me the leverage to negotiate an equity position in a production or upstream partnership.

Crude oil, more specifically kerosene from the Turkmen coastline, had been traded, refined and transported north into the Russian river system and west to Baku since the late 19th century. A further valued criterion of the Turkmen crude was that it contained extremely low sulphur. The low sulphur content added value which would counter the restricted cargo capacity, that the vessels were constrained by, due to the river and canal seasonal draft controls. My emerging business model would gain an additional net back, or value premium, from the combination of a free on-board (FOB) exporter and a cost inclusive of freight (CIF) seller of their own oil production from Turkmenistan to a western sales point. A premium that had the potential to crystallise a significant gain through an incremental value chain: linking the production cost at the load port to the transported cost at the discharge port and, in my dreams, linking those to storage and onward transit cost against the final trade value per barrel at the western refinery gate. In industry parlance: an upstream (producer), midstream (transporter) and downstream (trader) owner-operator fiscal regime: a monopoly not seen in the hydrocarbon industry since the 1970s and, even then, principally within the US based Seven Sisters.

My Caspian Game Plan collated with my Olympic Oil and Gas technological and country report, and, supported by my personal country experience, had, I felt, a sound commercial and politically risk-adjusted message to those with astute hands in the industry who sought the next wonder opportunity. The problem, as I had neither personal nor external financial support, was to ensure that those hands were, ultimately, also holding my hand. Not only is the hydrocarbon industry extremely competitive and strewn with the remains of lost leaders and grateful recipients of exclusive knowledge, but it is also thick with emerging political dictators, despotic leaders and strongmen that would wipe the floor with any messenger. I had read of the singularly lonesome track of the television pioneer, J. Logie Baird, who became easy prey for copyright exploitation and corporate raiders. I took a mental note of his circumstances and, whilst not in Mr Logie Baird's league, did likewise and withheld the detailed factual data of my priority information from circulation until my position within the Game was secured.

I continued to meet socially at Christian's Saville Row office where lunch and drinks were always on offer. Sadly, Anthony was not to be seen or mentioned as the pair had fallen out over a debt owing despite their long friendship. Anthony's failure to repay was a great disappointment to Christian's Danish principles. I knew that Christian had made him a loan for a six-figure sum the previous summer which confirmed my loose understanding of the personal problems, both family and business, that Anthony was experiencing. It was on one of these casual occasions at Christian's office that two shipping executives, Michael and Simon visited, without notice, to discuss a tanker chartering business matter. With interest, I observed the manner and style of the business conversation unfolding before me. I noted how Simon would be direct, coarse to the point of threatening, over a point that Michael would then take over and embellish amongst imagery of a gracious socially acceptable event (which made me completely lose the plot) in order to soften the accusation. Their dramatics amused and surprised me, as the point of business at hand neither merited nor resulted in their getting satisfaction, as Christian was obviously not the offending party.

When normal relations resumed, I was noticed and introduced to the pair along with a brief summary of my activities in and around the Caspian which, if nothing else, seemed to have a stabilising effect on the situation. Coincidentally, it transpired that the pair, in their broader business portfolio, had recently entered into a ship management and charter business for a Romanian freezer class vessel fleet which, given the accelerating demise and influence of the former Soviet Union, offered opportunities that were, like mine, becoming the norm for London. Apart from the timing, there was no immediate overlap between us and they left. I was taken by their 'nice cop/nasty cop' routine.

Within weeks of that introductory meeting at Christian's office, a second indirect connection was surprisingly made. Simon, being a keen fisherman, had travelled to Ireland to a beat along the banks of the Blackwater River as a guest of my sister, Roisin, and her London city financial analyst husband. At lunch, he talked about his eastern shipping fleet operations which prompted Roisin to comment on her brother's business (or hopes thereof) in the Caspian region. In need of social fighter cover she invited our brother Adrian, then living locally, who had had a brief career in shipping, to come for dinner. Adrian made the trip and, over the meal, Simon made the association with me back in Christian's London office.

The following weeks brought real traction to the business plan. Resulting from Adrian's introduction to Simon in Ireland, a lunch meeting with Michael and Simon was arranged where I presented an overview of my business plan. Intentionally, I disclosed only limited details. Further meetings introduced a potential business structure and union of their shipping contacts in their geographic sector with my detailed business plan, which could crystallise into a joint company. It was a significant step, predicated on their relationship with the Russian River-Sea shipping company, Volgotanker. The Volgotanker introduction was their core-contributing asset to my business plan and would enable me to commence the initial stages of an operation. With the contribution of my business game plan, sweat equity and recently acquired personal representative company, Balor Holding Limited, I negotiated (from a relatively weak position) a final net-free carried equity holding to 16%, inclusive of my travel costs, in a Cypriot registered group to be known as Sumo Transportation and Trading Limited (STT). Michael and Simon's dominant position and interest was to form a prevailing bias in the partnership that was weighted towards a midstream (transporting) and potential downstream (marketing) business model.

Despite my contacts that were to yield the cargo, there was no mention of the upstream (hydrocarbon producing) objective in the company manifesto despite my business plan proposal, possibly or, in fact, probably *because* it was seen by them as a pipe dream. My upstream dream was dependent on events which, although were unfolding at the time, I was not able to promote to my advantage in the equity holding ratio as their understanding of the upstream industry business was as limited as my next steps were unknown.

Further traction came with Adrian's introduction of Tacoma. Their appearance was beneficial not just for my business plan but also to his future. Coincident with the shipping developments over this period, the annual International Petroleum meeting in London took place. Over that week, a congenial pair of Geneva based product traders caught up with Adrian for old time's sake. Adrian invited me along, as he considered my Caspian business plan to be of interest to the traders. The chat with the founder and partner from Tacoma Trading soon blossomed into a discussion about the 'Game Plan' which would enthral most all traders, as a European based trader would wish to source and benefit from product or crude cargoes from the Former Soviet Union. The idea of having an asset on the ground in the Caspian with such a diverse business model and objective was just perfect for their aspirations. In as many weeks another foundation was laid as the Tacoma principle, Andy Dossenbach, a personification of the perfect Swiss business man – multilingual, of gentle manner, both considerate and thoughtful with impeccable taste – extended a hand of cooperation by offering to assist me with the preparation of any crude purchase contract and future financing Letters of Credit for the crude, from either or both of the sellers, Larmag or Bridas. This, of course, was like morning birdsong to me, as it was an area where I had absolutely no knowledge or experience. Adrian was immediately enrolled into the Tacoma Trading team as their 'Caspian and Russian' broker with the specific purpose to support me. Whilst I was pleased with the developments, I was also envious of Adrian's salaried financial security, which I longed for but seemed to evade me, as others had the perception that I was receiving financial remuneration from my own singular activities.

I did not have long to dwell on my sorry economic state, as the Sumo team was migrating to Cyprus where a meeting with the President of Volgotanker – the largest registered shipping fleet in the world (on paper and in dry dock) – had been convened following exchanges and offers of technical and financial assistance between the Sumo freezer fleet manager and Volgotanker repair managers at the Ruse ship yards in Bulgaria. The former wishing to learn more of the Russian register requirements and the latter hoping to understand western ship financing. The encounter provided the entrance to both the personality and the energy holding Volgotanker in play and, soon, the force that would propel the mass of both Sumo and Volgotanker into a common orbit: a Buddha-like man by the name of Andrey Pannikov, President of Urals Trading. Andrey was a man that could operate the 'pile driver' for any future foundations required; a figure as wide as he is high with cunning, good Jewish looks: retired 1st March 1991 rank Colonel from the KGB aged 41y.o. He actively participated in the Soviet bureaucratic and business transition to a private enterprise state, holding a nominee position throughout the last commercial active years of the Soviet national oil export group within the Soviet Oil Ministry, known as Soyous-Nefte-Export. He was a cofounder of numerous world-class oil and gas ventures including, but not limited to, Urals Trading. He resided in Cyprus with his wife and family, and Moscow with his friends and colleagues. Andrey would later tell me that you can never retire from the KGB.

Andrey took an interest in the meetings and, after formal talks, was prepared to continue a side-line discussion alone with me on my Caspian 'Game Plan'. He was intrigued if not convinced, but liked the detail and knowledge forthcoming from our chat which prompted him to arrange a Volgotanker 'Letter of Understanding' from President Strokin to supply a crude oil tanker vessel on request to Sumo Transportation & Trading when a cargo was ready with a stem (loading) date. This letter was gold dust to me.

Back in the UK, I reluctantly agreed to my partner Sumo's wish that I move into their London based office in Folgate Street, which involved a costly commute and the selection of a different desk on a daily basis. It did however prove highly educational as I learnt, through osmosis, the important differences between time, voyage and bare-boat charter contracts along with shipping terminology, operations and maritime personnel detail. My upstream geophysics and geology days at Chevron, United Geophysical and in Australia became a distant haze. Nobody thought to even question my past or experience, never imagining that sitting amongst their ship management team was someone with such practical experience in the world of oil and gas exploration. It was into my isolated, noisy and chaotic environment that one man would come and make my working life a joy, a proverbial carpet ride, as he appeared as if by the rub of the bottle – Sharif (aka Akhtar Sharif).

Sharif (36), a travel agent's ticket deliveryman, was quick to inform me that he had recently arrived from Bangladesh to join his English born wife and had a British passport pending. My interest rose immediately when he demonstrated his geographic familiarity with my destination, Ashgabat, and drew my total attention on his claim to both speak Russian and possess knowledge of Russian shipping from his time training as a Russian sea cadet in the Black Sea fleet. Sharif politely questioned my needs and intended course of action in Turkmenistan, which led me to give him a quick historical overview of the last year. Sensing a bond and definite need for such a lad, I took the opportunity to immediately offer him a job, although without pay as I had no budget and was myself unpaid. Sharif agreed. On securing a second ticket following a discussion with my partners and on the arrival of Sharif's UK passport, we both set off for Ashgabat days later.

Sharif learnt the 'fast airport transfer, light luggage, cheap end' style of travel that was my existence when the destination was Turkmenistan. All visas, including onward travel to Moscow, were acquired on arrival at the airport in Ashgabat and accommodation arranged on a local call. Sharif always presented his natural, friendly, obliging and all absorbing cheerful manner en route. My custom, on arrival, was to travel the six-hour drive by local car to Nebit Dag and there make unannounced visits to Arazov and his team at the regional office of Turkmeneft. I would update them on my achievements and objectives and, in return, they would show genuine hospitality by opening new dossiers of technical information in a casual manner that seemed to me to be an act of dismissal and liberation from their overbearing Soviet backgrounds.

Following Arazov's advice and counsel, I had accepted that, given their close presidential relations, the Argentinian company, Bridas, were not interested in a third-party sale of crude. Their intent was self-evident as their own man, Diego Lynch Maquee, was commanded with the task of chartering a fleet of tankers. Diego could not be faulted for his dedication but sadly would never get to load one vessel with Bridas crude, as their contract was court-bound within three years of signing with the contractor defaulting and a claim of force majeure paralysing any further progress ad infinitum. Before all these sad events played out, I did, however, spend a wonderful afternoon eating goat and drinking Turkmen vodka close to the Iranian border with Diego. Whether it was the culinary mix or the amount I consumed or both, I became comatose and was brought unconscious by car to Anna's flat in Ashgabat. Already, Sharif, through his underground network and contacts, had found local help to assist Anna who, being a granny in her dotage and well acquainted with the poor standard of local vodka, revived me amongst soft spoken Russian. The next day we both set off for the Caspian coast and the Larmag camp to meet with their general director – Martin Lewis.

Martin had by then heard of my name but not my technical background from local Turkmen or, specifically, from Arazov. Martin was a sensible, straight talking likeable Dutchman, without an ego or an arrogant fibre to his body, who accepted me as he would any shipping and trading character with whom he could do business. My letter from Volgotanker sealed a deal in principle but the financial details would need to be authorised by his Amsterdam head office. I took the opportunity to make a tour of their facilities. In the all-important canteen and mess rooms, I could not help but note the large number of expats making up the excessive work force in comparison to local personnel. I saw the overloaded presence of expatriates as a common error made by operators with limited or no previous experience in the upstream business. In remote locations, operations experience dictated that the 'thin end of the wedge' approach was required to control cost and demonstrate productive team work before growth in the cost base and personnel could follow. An excess of expats was a basic error that fuelled contempt, not only from the national host and ministry, but from the local administrative, technical and blue-collar community who could do the same or a better job for a tenth of the cost. Within four years of the Effective Date, Larmag would sell their non-performing project to experienced operator, Dragon Oil.

At Larmag's head office in Amsterdam, I followed the draft of the crude oil purchasing agreement between Sumo Transportation & Trading and Larmag Turkmenistan that Andy Dossenbach at Tacoma had both drafted and kindly spent time tutoring me on, which seemed to cover my ignorance sufficiently. Over the complex terminology and detail of the pricing formulae, I was able to conference call Andy into the proceedings, which delivered a calm and commercial result.

On my arrival back in London, the delivery of a crude oil purchase Agreement with Larmag sent Michael and Simon plus Sumo Transportation & Trading into higher orbit. I took the opportunity to request and grant a salary for Sharif, my No.1 employee, who was making all the Russian translations, voyage charter logistics and clearing our path of any sundry obstacle or local issue that continued to appear. The agreement heralded the start of the next exponential grind and a 20th century first: putting my theoretical business model into an operational and commercial business. The domino effect of correlating standard western shipping documentation into former Soviet Union equivalent, in particular Caspian Sea related activity, was audible. Western underwriting cargo insurance and guaranteed out-turn insurance terms required a quality and quantity cargo inspector which, in turn, would require a local customs inspector with a full suite of regulatory stamps anointing western certification, which at that moment in time, did not exist along the eastern load ports of the Caspian Sea.

The business belief and relationship between Michael, Simon and I also ascended apace. Their unexpected rise in the oil trading and transportation business in the former Soviet Union justifiably inflated their business credentials and interest amongst their community. With a signed contract, introductions to their numerous finance institutions both in Geneva and London followed post haste. Time was both wasted and enjoyed through interesting meetings with London 'underworld' financiers, whose interest and surprise at being introduced and presented to by the technologist of a natural resource-based business in a country they had never heard of was theatrical. One meeting in particular, held in a Dickensian styled large office with equally well-dressed frock-coated office staff fronted by a distinguished grey-haired squire, was a gem. 'Black Jack Delayll', a well-known commercial developer and loan shark amongst the London East-End community, was bemused to the point of becoming sentimental with disbelief that he was being offered such a high risk, long term, subterranean project located so far outside his manor. So thoughtful, he gently took me aside and mentioned that he had not seen the sight of the crucifixion but that, on this day, he believed that here before him was the closest yet to that vision. I gave him a most congenial thank you for his time and concern over my wellbeing. I soon realised that he and my Game Plan, which had made strides forward, were being used and seen as a Victorian gore show, taken from office to office with the sole objective of elevating my partners' business integrity. Nevertheless, the project was at a place that it could be seen, if not visited, and as Diana was first to mention then, and continued to remind me over the forthcoming years, Michael and Simon were the only business partnership that gave me and my Game Plan a chance.

From spring into early summer, Sharif maintained a daily vigilance conversing with Volgotanker in Samara, assisted by Charles Clancy from the Sumo chartering department on the floor above. I made pioneering visits to the trading floor of the Lloyds Insurance market clasping a map of the Caspian region along with my crude oil purchasing contract, where I roamed from syndicate table to syndicate table explaining my requirements and project opportunity before eventually meeting the team from Marsh that were prepared, interested and mind-boggled enough to underwrite our activities. Similarly, I took to the streets of Mayfair to find a trading house with an associated commodity inspection operation that was prepared to mobilise into a new area, to conduct and build a business.

As the logistical pieces and Voyage Charter agreement fell into shape, along with the issue of timing of the 'stem date' (loading date of the ship) from Larmag, there then appeared the not unforeseeable issue of making the pre-payment to Vogotanker for the vessel. It was at this juncture I found that Michael and Simon were not as forthcoming with money as they were with their business acquaintances. This realisation exposed my rather naïve faith and belief in people, especially those in business, when I had preferred not to scratch the surface or seek out detail through due diligence. There was a weakness in my understanding of my partners which, in the interest of brevity and speed, left me sucker-punched. Through my eyes, their business partnership had a bipolar quality: to me, Michael was vain, had the bigger ego but was honest, while Simon had a threatening demeanour at times and showed perfidious character traits – often disingenuous on numerous issues, most frequent of those being payment terms. Such aspects of their characters would continue to worry me as I became ever more integrated into their, or our, partnership.

With the stem date fast approaching and the immediate requirement for finance, I was propelled further into the wonderful world of trade finance and its individual creative form through Andy at Tacoma in Geneva, from whom I had continued taking advice in learning the art of trading crude cargo, and who showed his brilliance with a back-to-back 'transportation cost and crude purchase' Letter of Credit that took the finance liability for the transaction away from us and STT. This was indeed the answer and one that highlighted to me Michael and Simon's financial limitations, a realisation to which they took offence. Future relations between the two parties were poor from that moment on and remained so throughout our long association.

I arrived into the searing August heat of Ashgabat where I stayed again in the Soviet apartment with Granny Anna, but this time, I was in good health and had her kind invitation. Sharif remained in London to co-ordinate the movement of the Volgoneft vessel and reported to me by phone at Anna's place, this being the only communication available to me. I spent my days re-reading Oscar Wilde's 'Picture of Dorian Grey' and some choice Dickens which Anna had on her shelf. It was customary furniture apparel in the Soviet home to have a library of works of, if possible, Pushkin and Dickens, their works being a sign of good proletariat standards and seniority. Anna prepared the basic Turkmen foods of salads, soups and pelmeni, which were all that I required given the persistent heat throughout the day and night. I would accompany Anna into the local market where, on one occasion, I caught a glimpse of wonderful Turkmen, if not Central Asian, ingenuity in action: a seated salesman surrounded by his cardboard boxes full of broken lightbulbs. 'Broken lightbulbs for sale' I performed for Anna? She explained with difficulty that one of the benefits from a government work place was the prohibited opportunity to replace a working bulb with a broken bulb which could be brought home. This racket gave me a deep insight into the mind and the extreme economics in play with which the people must wrestle.

On the sixth day, I got the call from Sharif that the vessel was due to arrive within 24 hours to present the NOR (notice of readiness) that would trigger the charter party contract and, shortly thereafter, contractually commence the Lay-can period (contractual loading period usually up to and including five days). However, Sharif also mentioned that the Volgotanker management had been made aware through their post-Soviet system news wire, that there were political issues abounding around the lifting of crude oil out of the country and that the president was agitated by the lack of national production and shortage of crude at their refinery gate at the Turkmenbashi refinery. This was a concern, but not an overt one, as at that time I was running on optimism.

My and the vessel's arrival at the Larmag camp and Cheleken terminal generated interest as, by then, most understood the need to make the first commercial sale of equity-produced crude oil. I was delighted to find that they, like me, had a 'Sharif', only theirs was called Tim. Tim Singay was a Russian lad with extreme exuberance, confidence and energy. He immediately took control of logistical discussions between the vessel's captain, the 'harbour master' (the same as customs) and the battery tank farm from where the crude was stored. I stood on the wooden jetty thinking of the young Hesperus and the short distance that existed between my dream and the vessel, being only 100 meters away on the moorage berth. It was all so close, so real and so extraordinary in the context of the last eighteen months. Then, and without notice, the vessel pulled anchor, turned north and steamed away. The contract was off. The president had spoken. I stood on the jetty, feeling the deck burning from the sun and overwhelmed by the belief that my Game Plan, career and family's financial future had vanished along with that vessel, then heading over the horizon.

The return flight was going to be a lonely affair remembering past failures: *On getting back into the office in Pasadena after the scout and bid preparation for Somalia where there was a notable change in the atmosphere. It soon became apparent why my earlier 30%IIR (Internal Rate of Return) winning bids were not being accepted by our corporate owner Bendix: we were up for sale. The news around the office was that by the following Wednesday afternoon at 2pm EST, should a private sale not be approved, United Geophysical Corporation was to commence the process of listing on a public stock exchange. This excited the senior professionals who along with the long-term secretarial class became extremely giddy with excitement as they all fairly owned and participated in the share stock plan and had done so for many years. Talk over cruise brochures and home improvement magazines became the norm. Either way they would benefit, which I genuinely thought was a wonderful expression of capitalism. But a listing on the New York Stock Exchange was not to be as an industry competitor, Seiscom Delta from Houston and led by a lawyer CEO, offered a purchase bid of $70m that was immediately accepted by the Bendix Corporation. It was only hours later that the white-collar suited brigade appeared and took over the office communications much like a coup in a sub-Saharan city. I enjoyed the moment as the cigar toting CEO sat with his feet on my desk relaying how 'it was God who had told him to buy the company'. I repeatedly offered to light his cigar before realising that he didn't smoke, and asked him whether God had bothered to relay to him the counter-cultures of his two principle clients: Amoco and Texaco. United was loved and contracted by Amoco throughout the continental USA for its no-nonsense get-the-job-done-well-without-fuss approach while Texaco, the exact opposite, would contract only Seiscom Delta for its white-collar city-style computer-driven technological appearance, never United. The result of the merger was that, within days of the announcement, both* *majors had terminated all their onshore US continental contracts with the new company – Seiscom Delta United.*

Akhtar Sharif, Tim Singay and myself

Chapter 4
A Man and His Dog

I made a very recognisable sweeping or washing of the hair action as I moved through the custom line at departures later that August for the red-eye flight to Istanbul. Confused, or amused, the Turkmen custom official didn't address the six rather heavily bandaged plastic bottles holding black liquid that passed through the hand luggage conveyor belt and onto the plane. Tim had been brilliant in my state of defeat. We entered the battery tank farm at Okarem, collected the only available bottles from the waste bin and decanted the oil which had been lifted from within the tank into the buckets we dipped through rusted-out holes on the top of the battery tanks. Without bottle caps, we used heavy plastic tape to secure the six litre bottles and, bottled oil in tow, I set off for Ashgabat. I placed the bag containing the bottles in the last empty overhead luggage rack of the Turkish Airlines 737, which also happened to be above the only passenger wearing a smart white jacket, and then went to my seat and immediately slept the deep sleep of the weary.

As the crew put the cabin in order and prepared to land at Istanbul, I got the first whiff of kerosene. Most would accept the plane or location as the explanation, as none would consider that it was crude oil leaking in the hand luggage rack. As the gentleman in the white jacket rose to disembark, a stark black streak divided his back, with more drops taking range. In the immigration hall, the bag was leaking profusely, with many joining the dots to me moving swiftly through the lines awaiting a visa. I moved through the arrivals hall and out into the polluted air of the airport without a visa thanks to my Australian passport where a visa-waiver existed to honour historic relations between the two countries and commemorate the 75th anniversary of the Anzac invasion. In the departures shopping area, I bought a bottle of whiskey which came in a stout plastic bag suitable for a further six bottles and got closure. My call to Andy with the request that the crude oil be taken to his Assay team in Amsterdam (plus airfare) was the best course that following day. There, in Amsterdam, the team received a most unusual package containing an international oil sample but rested their case when, on cleaning, the seventh bottle appeared to be a bottle of Jameson.

In personal and commercial terms, the whole trip had been a failure that had left me very much back in my own corner, alone with Sharif. At least the trip had provided the first modern sample of Turkmenistan crude to provide a product assay result. Hopefully, and despite my possible exclusion, that result would be the basis for further interest and, on the next occasion, a real commercial success.

For the following weeks, I remained in my bunker in the belief that the support from Michael and Simon, together with Volgotanker, would evaporate. What I could not see, as those from the touchline could, was that my singular efforts over the past six months had put my Game Plan and teamwork together at zero capital cost to support a new business plan. Also, there had been a minimum or zero loss to Volgotanker as their Volgoneft vessel had been re-chartered to load from the Turkmenbashi refinery within hours of departure from my location, and, apart from Tacoma's bank line charge, there had been no large cost or credit lines actually opened. In effect, my wounded pride aside, there had been no financial damage to any of the supporting players. This silver lining grew ever more brilliant upon connecting with and updating Brian at Monument Oil, who took the opportunity to advance the Game Plan project with an update of events to Tony Craven Walker, CEO and Founder of Monument. My recent failure, although a failure, had proved the reality of the business plan which, together with the upstream oil field data from my earlier meetings with Brian, could allow the CEO and Monument staff to evaluate a real proposition of a midstream/upstream operation and partnership.

The relationship moved very quickly, as I understood that Brian, ever the explorer seeking out a new direction, had been keeping a close watch over my activities since our first reunion the previous year. This was useful as he had already taken a view on the regional or project petroleum system and technical risk from my brochure, leaving only one topic to be explored, a topic which I knew normally dampened or terminated any discussion of a business nature in this geographic region – political risk. To my happy surprise, Brian must have already overcome that obstacle through his own understanding or review of my recent activities, as the subject never arose. He had taken his view and understood the value of shipping control. Brian worked alongside his colleague and petroleum engineer, Atul Gupta. I was immediately impressed by Atul's silent, thoughtful deliberations, which were interrupted only by short yet precise responses to important issues on any given conversational topic. He would summarise the position and the necessary next steps well, but, as I could see as with most all of my peers, there lacked street-wise experience. Following the initial series of meetings with Tony, the plan was hatched for the three of us – Brian, Atul and myself – to make a reconnaissance evaluation visit to Turkmenistan.

It felt different from all my earlier trips to Turkmenistan, as being with a group of likeminded hydrocarbon explorers gave me a rare sense of security – a security that I had not felt since my days with Chevron in Canada. It was a good feeling that I am sure glowed out of me during my introduction to the Turkmen ministry personnel and, in particular, to Arazov, when we eventually reached Nebit Dag town. I was particularly delighted to make the introduction of 'real' technologists representing a 'real' western oil company which had 'real' hard currency money to invest and which could compensate Arazov for the events eighteen months earlier. Brian, a lad motivated by social welfare responsibilities, made broad strides to divert our conversations to include not just the technological requirements, both above and below the surface, but also to understand the social and demographic needs of the region.

Our arrival really gave Arazov the sense that the cavalry had at long last ridden over the hill. In presenting the investment opportunities within the region and, more importantly, knowing the political status of each and every national asset, Arazov politely reduced the margin of interest away from the offshore back to an area highlighted by the Burun Field. He was quick to point out that the Burun field was not a major producing field in comparison to its peers, positioned as it was at the eastern and terminal end of the Caspian Basin petroleum system fairway. His lesson broadly explained that this world class system which supported the prolific production, from Baku in the west under the Caspian Sea to onshore western Turkmenistan, remained under-explored. Arazov made particular note of the Turkmen region and the shallow oil-bearing formations in particular which, in his view, were extremely commercial further to the east. He convincingly described the Burun field as one with the least exploited fields, on a cumulative production per well basis to date and with good exploration potential upside; he therefore wanted to promote the field for future investment. Arazov concluded that the Burun field might be the runt, but a runt that was best suited for the Monument team on his listed principles and appraised view of the field's size and potential. He wasn't 100% correct, but was not wrong either, as we would go ahead and prove.

Following a brief scout of the Burun Field by car then continuing west along the Cheleken road, mostly covered by drifting sand, we reached the Larmag camp close to the shore of the Caspian Sea. It was Brian and Atul's turn to get that feeling of security, as they felt embraced by the lavish expatriate surroundings and facilities which I had long given up. I got that sense of having brought the beautiful girls to the party who then left you at the door as they saw the better dressed and moneyed set. It was totally foreseeable that the Larmag reception placed me on the side of the service provider as, to date, all my past visitations had been as the transportation and crude purchasing agent which, to them, equated to a second-class oil citizen, a status I had accepted back in the seismic service days. My personal confidence, following the let-down of my previous visit, was growing again as I knew that I was being dealt cards for a potential winning hand from the international oil and gas pack. A hand that would trump the geo-political stagnation of western investment in this eastern hemisphere and, with a few years yet to play out, yield my ongoing family risk a worthy result.

The Larmag operational team were delighted to provide the Monument visitors with a full, hands-on tour of the offshore and onshore facilities. The former came as a total shock to the pair of Morecombe Bay operators for the extremely poor standards of safety, deprivation and sheer rust of the fifty plus year oil structures. The view over the waters to submerged or half raised rigs, which had met their end through blow-out fires or submarine earth movements, caused many silent moments as one reflected on the lives lost. I made the unemotional observation that the oil field was more of a liability on top of an asset and that the best opportunity for cash flow could be generated from the sale of scrap metal. On departure, the Monument pair paid likewise lip service to the extreme number of expatriate personnel present, the cost and seemingly insurmountable contractual, logistical and operational issues which the Larmag team would soon have to confront.

An alternative site visit would have been to the Argentinian Bridas residence facility in Ashgabat. This was not on offer however, as the company was confronting presidential objections and contractual problems over their contract performance. This was not a surprise as I had concluded a year earlier, from my review of the Aziz contract which was similar, that both operations would suffer administrative and legal difficulties over the oil pool division and accounts. I was happy not to pursue a meeting as I did not want our journey to become politically tarnished through association, something which I knew to be a very Soviet phenomenon.

Concurrent with the Monument trip in Turkmenistan, Michael and Simon had been on a tour to the western Black Sea port of Constanta to oversee the dockyard repair and maintenance ongoing with their Romanian joint venture Reefer fleet. As always, I had learnt from office conversations and osmosis that the pair's constant bridge-burning and need for new avenues of finance had led to an in-flight conversation with a solitary, wandering American by the name of Richard Sobel, a London based financier from Baring Asset Management, and Michael's Russian speaking and extremely competent PA, Jocelyn Graham Wilson. What started as a pleasant in-flight chat-up line soon turned to business that brought Michael and Simon into a discussion about their Romanian Reefer Fleet ship management business and expanded, as required, to include a synopsis of the Game Plan. This had Richard immediately intrigued and wanting to learn more (as I learnt later from Jocelyn), but Michael's pitch and progress was rather stumped when Richard commented that he would not invest in any project, especially those 'man and his dog' shows or outfits. They agreed to arrange a meeting between 'their' technologist and project manager and Richard in London as soon as possible.

I just happened to be in town that autumnal Saturday morning and willing to walk my cocker spaniel to the prescribed meeting point in Hyde Park. I was initially disdainful of their request to meet up with a 'Richard', it being a weekend. Not far from the Kensington Park children's playground and close to the fairytale tree, I heard clearly a New York accent cry out, "Oh my God! It's a man with his dog." That immediately impacted on our meeting and subsequent excellent relationship. Richard's initial decision to invest through a private equity fund under Barings management would, over time, develop into a Baring nominee portfolio being the largest shareholder and beneficiary from the Game Plan. We discussed the details of an embryonic legal draft that would establish a formal partnership between the Sumo group and Monument Oil. Rightly or wrongly, I had yet to discuss this draft bidding agreement with Michael and Simon for fear that they may intercede and disrupt my negotiation.

The Bidding Agreement: a document that would position Sumo as a 50% beneficiary to purchase any foreign held equity resulting from negotiation on the rights to explore and produce within the existing Burun Field, in the Balkanabad region of Western Turkmenistan. That all the costs in establishing that result, would be paid for by Monument Oil.

This agreement was a massive commercial step forward and an ace card dealt. Sumo was to maintain and continue to develop the transportation and export system as it best saw fit, whilst Monument was to bring in the equity crude oil agreement. For me and Sumo, this was sight of the Holy Grail, as to reach that objective in the hydrocarbon industry parties must work together in partnership – a partnership between equals – and the parties to my draft agreement were unique in comparison to any standard industry agreements of a similar nature.

The Bidding Agreement was signed without fanfare with Monument Oil. However, the significance and commercial importance was not lost on my partners, Simon and Michael, as they considered the document to be an invitation to a series of banquet lunches and evening dinners. A more sinister realisation became apparent to me as I saw them realise that my objective in the Game Plan was going to work.

The implication of this vision for STT altered the shareholder atmosphere. I was sensitive over my equity holding like a hunter-and-the-hunted instinct. They lost no time and propelled themselves, along with their business profile, into yet another orbit. They raised and broadened their new identity as the new wonders of the London upstream oil and gas world, the majority of whom had no experience of their Jonah-style fiscal or working practice. They ingratiated themselves into Monument Oil's higher management with lavish offers of lunches and dinners. They breezed through the upper echelon of corporate investment bankers who, like Richard, were searching for that hot ticket and a position to partner a workable Former Soviet primary production project verified and managed by a well-respected London based resource company.

It was very noticeable from these early partner meetings and onwards that I was not viewed as an equal, but rather a technician under their control and business acumen. It was the start of a long period of psychological and mild paranoia-related stress for me as I lost control of both the information flow of the project on the upstream development to Monument and the half-proven shipping and transportation or midstream development which had then entered Michael and Simon's domain. I had to maintain my place at the table. The Game was moving into very high stakes, as recent events had proven the practical and commercial potential of my plan, even if it had no proven value yet.

Michael and Simon saw correctly the current state of play as a hugely credible promotional act and an opportunity for them to leverage their debts, shore up their thin cash flows and broaden their supply lines as the news of their new business opportunity was broadcast. I was only too aware that an orderly line of invitations from presentable companies would benefit the Turkmen resource sector and STT. In contrast, to broadcast the news was only going to draw the flies from within the local upstream sector towards the low hanging fruit in western Turkmenistan, upsetting the primitive commercial balance in the region. This was a country that had over a short space of time since its independence been seen as off-limits to the establishment due to its lack of export infrastructure.

Michael and Simon moved quickly to promote and circulate draft documentation to commence the legal incorporation process which would connect the two loose keystones that made up Sumo with the boulders of Volgotanker, Urals Trading and the perfect white-collar party of Baring Asset Management. Monument Oil, while totally ignorant of the weak commercial bond between the Russian and other parties, were invited, in principle, to meet their Russian counterparts. It was hoped their very presence would enhance the Sumo bonding process and convince the Monument team that they had a solid amalgam of a partner. With Michael's bravado and the suggestion of an open cheque book, he arranged for a five-day informal 'conference' to be held in Moscow where each party (covering their own costs) would gather, meet and get to know each other. Amongst the group were others invited for gravitas to act as satellite-interested parties taken from the London marine insurance and ship broking sectors. President Strokin from Volgotanker was given the highest honours and privileges along with my Russian equivalent and acolyte, Andrey Pannikov. Andrey remained aloof throughout the numerous meals, yet did not miss the point or the opportunity to converse with Richard who was fluent in Russian, as was his Moscow-based companion Mike Calvey. Both Mike and Richard had worked together previously with the EBRD bank in London and before at Salomon Brothers. Their value and position in the project was by then assured, as it was clear that they had the purse (and therefore the answers) to most all of the Volgotanker problems.

In the company of the Monument executives, the theme was collaboration and domination of the region, whilst beyond their earshot the focus was resolution of the issue of Volgotanker's finance requirement: new finance was required for fleet refurbishment and the replacement of salvageable vessels with new builds and these were problems for which neither President Strokin nor Andrey Pannikov had a solution. President Strokin, in particular, did not see the answer lying in their participation in an oil production project in a tuberculosis ridden old colony of their recent lost empire. The Monument team remained oblivious to the fractious issues and, like good young tourists, befriended all the parties and found the whole introduction much to their liking and above their expectations.

I could sense there existed between the four key players numerous cultural and divergent issues with only one binding solution, which Michael showed the good business sense to address. Volgotanker required western financial instruments to repair and, more adventurously, construct new builds for their antique fleet; Urals, Andrey's Russian trading company, required a fleet of vessels to support its inland Russian waterways product trading operation; Michael and Simon 'needed' to be part of a big project; and, Baring Asset Management wanted to invest in the Former Soviet Union. However, Barings did not want to invest solely through a loan mechanism overseen by Russian management. Michael presented the Sumo Group as the obvious vehicle to transact the business, it being an experienced ship management company and presentable finance force with the Game Plan which had the capacity to add spice and upside to the project all whilst under a western management. This was a group that could be restructured to satisfy the business requirements of the parties through share ownership as well as meet, amongst other factors, debt and collateral obligations within a western managed joint stock company.

In theory, to create a joint stock company between the players that would provide stock to assign collateral was an exceptionally good plan. The value of that stock would be determined by any number of factors, the result of the Bidding Agreement being just one that both Richard and Mike Calvey viewed highly while Volgotanker remained mute. The structure proposed would commit Volgotanker to the ship requirements of the Game Plan, whether interested or not, as they would have their funding requirements covered.

Michael and Simon, whilst maintaining the upstream potential, saw the outcome as their beneficial slush fund, comparable to a ship management agreement and in a business style best suited to their elusive practices. Andrey and Urals Trading were content as long as Volgotanker confirmed their supply of good vessels. I shared my opinion with Richard, namely that the proposal reflected and solved the prevailing issues, but I continued to be concerned over the decision to allow Michael and Simon management and control of the cash. Richard disagreed, feeling instead that my concern was based upon personal and irrational bias against them, as was his prerogative. However, over the next twelve months, he would understand from whence my concerns emanated.

****

The weekly living with Pete Gathings in the rental accommodation in Houston was not going to work. Pete's waking 5am TV news broadcasts, concurrent both up and down stairs through the paper-thin Houston dry sealed walls, was driving me mad. The demoralising corporate take-over, draining weekly commute from LA to Houston and lack of business direction had taken its toll. The past President of United Geophysical, Mike Clevenger, had not been invited to join Seiscom Delta United which was a turn of events that proved profitable for him, as he remained in Pasadena to join the remnants of the United Geophysical technical division spun off many years earlier and then a new listed public company in its own right – Geophsicalsystems Corporation. Mike and I stood in line for a table at the Oil Club lunch only to be seated beside the divine lawyer and CEO of SeisCom Delta United. With my next move exposed, I would be forced to sell my soul to Mike for any position on offer. It didn't matter as I knew that I was not staying, despite Diana being then pregnant and applying for Houston jobs. Following that lunch, I became the typical itinerant service oilman: lives in LA, has a deposit on a house in Houston but is moving to work in Australia with a pregnant wife.

Brian, Atul and myself offshore on a Larmag production platform

Chapter 5
A Crude Vision

Over that Christmas and into 1995, my sense of isolation amongst the project players and the project itself intensified. It had been two years since my first visit to Turkmenistan and, over that time, I had achieved the Bidding Agreement, cash for Anthony and Aziz but no core business plan value. My personal finances were running low from school and mortgage payments although, happily, the family spirits remained buoyant notwithstanding the lack of any holiday trips or luxuries.

I knew that I was being kept away from participating in agreeing the legal process and corporate structure that was earlier proposed. This was an obvious concern, as I was aware that it was being discussed at a professional level with a marine legal firm, Sinclair Roche & Temperley, that my equity was vulnerable and that it required my personal representation. Legal drafts were being reviewed without my knowledge and the third-party office rumour was that Michael and Simon considered my participation incremental or, worse, expendable. Disappointed as I was, there was soon a reason to be upbeat as news arrived from the most unexpected direction: the Turkmen President himself. Evolving from a rumour to a fact in a matter of weeks, the ban on crude exports six months earlier was lifted, leaving the way open for all parties to put the original business template back into action.

I left over the Holy Week with Sharif to travel to the Larmag camp to await the arrival of the Vogotanker, Volgoneft VN 220 vessel. Again, Andy had quickly put in play the Letters of Credit that would back-to-back the transportation costs due to Volgotanker, to the crude oil Purchase Agreement with Larmag and onto Tacoma itself as the end purchaser or, in this case, as an agent for the ELF Racing Team (ELF were to be the end users for the crude oil for their high-performance engines, given its unique qualities of low sulphur and high lubrication oil). The crude was to be discharged at the port of Varna, Bulgaria.

There was an air of excitement at the camp especially amongst those few who understood the importance of the arrival, the financial significance of its cargo and the origins of its journey. Sadly, Martin Lewis, the project manager, was on leave and replaced by a difficult, snobbish Brit who considered only a big company background of value and worthy of regard. For reasons that I put down to our corporate insignificance, he took a contemptuous attitude and instant dislike to me, Sharif and the entire export team. He forbade us access to the communication and logistics as, for him, vessel communication was treated as low priority. His contempt paled into insignificance as a real problem dawned: in spite of all the work preparation and logistical and financial instruments at play, there appeared the most basic of all basic problems as the vessel came alongside the jetty. The customs people were present, the crude battery tank on alert to pump and the president still willing, yet a simple inlet ring on the vessels pipe would not couple with the main outlet pipe from the land battery tank pipe! Over the years, between exports at this remote jetty, the Russian standard O-ring had changed. Two years of preparation and planning had to wait while Tim and Sharif went to look for a local blacksmith with the scales and measurement for the required main adaptor. Six hours and into darkness, the wait persisted. Eventually before dawn on that Easter Monday 1995, the gushing of crude oil through the simple pipe bound for the vessels bunker could be heard. It was a joyous sound which I followed, up and onto the vessel deck and leaning over the open bunker hole, in the dim light I could see, for the first time in my career, crude oil.

This was the real thing: an event that most exploration people in the industry over their career never get to see as their priority is to find it not to move it. Over 10 hours, the vessel loaded 2200 tonnes of crude oil. A total much less than expected and an amount that could be considered uncommercial but for the crude specifications which justified the voyage through to the western Black Sea port. The cargo amount limited due, in the captain's view, to the seasonal low draft of the canal as the snow melt water had yet to reach the southern Volga and Don rivers. I could hear the 'learning by experience' comments in blasts.

Into the afternoon's late winter sun, the vessel's silhouette steamed against the dimming yellow background view as best as any rust bucket could over contaminated water. A romantic view indeed with Sharif on board to note and view the Volga Don canal first hand. The super cargo, in the form of passenger 'Sharif', had not been expected by the captain who took authority from Samara to permit a foreigner on board as the Canal infrastructure was still considered by the Russian authorities a state secret! It was another first and a premiere that produced a premium as Sharif took elevation readings, photographs at each magnificent art deco designed lock gate, time charts and speed accounts through the canal to produce a hand drawn elevation cross section of the canal that remained our template and draft for that season and the next.

I was silent with jubilation at the success of this, the first western destined export of crude oil from Turkmenistan certainly since and maybe before the Soviet revolution. It was small time history, but history nonetheless, and for me, a massive moment – a moment that I wished I could share with my family. I travelled back by road through Nebit Dag to relate the event to Arazov (who knew all) and onto Ashgabat where my enthusiasm was diluted with the noise and information surrounding Monument's activities. My informants in the community had gone silent as we learnt that Latiffa, the translator from the Aziz team, had joined with the Monument team and given unfavourable reports of the earlier Aziz period. Mr Essanov, the minister, having presided along with his colleagues over the period of negotiation with Aziz and Anthony, was fully aware of my history and current participation. This risked ours, or my, standing, but it wasn't going to upset the recent events and would not be a hurdle, as our agreement with Monument was legal, tight and stood. Michael and Simon would sadly get to hear of the news through their buddies at Monument, which would give them further cause to distance me from the proceedings at hand.

I always made sure that on my return journey through Moscow I made contact with Andrey Pannikov and Mike Calvey, where possible, to individually give them an update which helped my state of mind as they were then growing in support, having digested the proposed corporate structure of the Newco that could be harnessed to the Game Plan's evolution. On each and every meeting with Andrey, I grew to understand that far from being the stereotype Soviet-styled bureaucrat that we learnt to accept through western dogma, Andrey was extremely intelligent, well read (particularly in western military history) and exceedingly well versed on western banking and legal documentation from his days in the Soviet oil export group. He had travelled widely in Europe, but not in the US or UK, as he was persona-non-grata due to internal testimony of his past commercial spying activities. His biggest concern, as I would have surmised from his immediate past, was trust. Trust in dealing with the partners that the cards had handed him. In this, I was able to be open as we both had a common interest in our respective equity holding and with our first crude lift and, even more than before, he by then held a positive belief in the upstream venture.

My overriding concern throughout this time and in the lead up to the tabling of the new Newco structure was my partnership within the Sumo structure. Since late the previous year, I had taken a view that I could not, and would not, persist in being a minority stakeholder within the Michael and Simon equity shareholding of Newco. This was an absolute must for me as I was convinced that the unpredictable tendencies of Simon would lead me to financial ruin or worse. I had to emerge into the Newco as a partner and shareholder in my own corporate name. This I knew would require funds to pay my proportional foundation capital contribution.

Outside this sphere of fractious facts and rumour came a wonderful diversionary bolt. Andy from Tacoma, who had gone quiet following another Turkmen Presidential decree and subsequent renewed ban on crude oil export, had nevertheless been kept abreast of developments, both corporate and operational, through my brother Adrian who maintained his Tacoma station in Russia and made periodic visits home to his family in Ireland. Andy was most interested in the news of the upstream development and, in particular, the Agreement with Monument Oil. He invited me to his Geneva office when next over, on banking and related business. I immediately turned this invitation into business necessity and went.

Andy's proposition was taken straight out of the Standard Oil club book of business development. As he made monthly visits to the suppliers and authorities along the numerous West African countries where from he lifted products, he would infrequently receive an approach to step up his role to an investor in that country's upstream development projects. It was essential to note, as I did, that the requests were being made directly from or through the finance minister, as that bureaucratic level had the authority to clear any hurdle given that the office had the invidious task of financing the president, king or chief and their respective wives. Up to that moment in response to each and every request Andy had kindly declined, based on the genuine excuse that it was an area of the business for which he simply did not have the technological knowledge. However, with our combined knowledge and his resulting observations of my model's achievements, Andy considered that it was time for Tacoma to make the gesture and offered for me to lead and participate in an upstream study to identify a licence block of my choosing, following a visit and overview. Andy wished that Adrian, also short of work given the presidential decree in Turkmenistan, would join me in the party to assist in practical matters. The initial trip would be a basic exploratory business development visit to his chosen West African Countries which may, on his appraisal, be the final trip. I agreed my deal with Andy for my work and time, for which again I went unpaid and, by instinct, it felt better to earn a 'sweat' equity interest 'carry' of up to 20% of Tacoma resulting net interest in the event of a licence(s) deal. I suggested to Adrian that he should do something similar, as my arrangement with Andy was mine alone.

I immediately fell in with his proposal, not just for the time available but also for the opportunity to expand the geographic play that my Game Plan could address. I did however remain slightly confused by the multi-tasking career persona that was emerging for me. Within the Monument sphere, I was less the geophysicist explorer and more the ship operations manager, as portrayed by my introduction from Tony Craven Walker, CEO of Monument Oil, to Richard Redmayne, his good friend and business acquaintance, as a 'Sea Captain' and my being directed by Redmayne to undertake a 'recce' into the Azov Sea port infrastructure and commercial asset.

Said recce was undertaken by Sharif and would prove most useful to the future development of the emergent shipping operation a few years later. Alongside Andy and his Tacoma Group, I was once again the academic with a position of exploration and business development. In Sumo, I had given up wondering on my current role other than being the butt of drunken post lunch conversations with financiers and others. At one in particular, a 'lady' dominantly put her feet on my desk to demonstratively express, in addition to her underwear, how she and her team were tasked to take over the Caspian! Obviously, after a good lunch with Simon.

Without doubt, the incorporation of Volgo Sumo Transportation and Trading Ltd (VSTT) under Cypriot law was a milestone development and a massive step forward to achieving the perceived unified interest of the parties. The company included shareholders Volgotanker 35%, Baring Asset Management 20%, Sumo (ex me) 20%, Ural Trading soon to be Sunfloat Trading 15% and my holding of 10% through Balor Holdings Limited. The company was financed up to the tune of $2million through the paid-up capital from each shareholder of $1.00 per new share issued. My requirement to raise $195,000 for Balor Holding became my major concern given that my net asset value at the time was certainly less. It was our mutual distrust of Michael and Simon that would drive Andrey to provide the funding for me and for my company to provide Andrey 'protection' through holding legal title to his equity shareholding. Unknown to me, Russian nationals were prohibited from holding foreign stock and he therefore had to look for sanctuary for his holding. The enjoyable times I had had with Andrey up until then would continue to flourish and benefit both parties, as each had a strong deed of trust for the other.

Our common objective had been achieved with the establishment of VSTT, a vehicle that could harness our energy and drive to meet and match the political, fiscal and competitive challenges that we would need to overcome. Soon thereafter, I joined a management meeting with Michael, the appointed Managing Director of VSTT, which rapidly became a departmental human resources interview. Rather than extend the hand of co-operation and appreciation for the joint and individual efforts over the past year, he seemed to take that opportunity to denigrate me in the eyes of all those involved, including the Monument team. His proposition and intention was to include me only as a part-time consultant as, in his words, 'I did not know the front end from the back end of a boat'. It was my hope and belief that this meeting was to focus on the future of the Game Plan and serve to defuse egos in the interest of moving the project into a higher gear: the proposition to involve VSTT in the embryonic Tacoma plan at a ground floor entrance price. I believe that it was Michael and his partner Simon's desire to take control of the injection of all further and future cash in this new western-controlled ship management company that blinded him to the bigger plan at that time.

Limited as my nautical knowledge was, and somewhat in agreement with the assertions of my limitations in that regard, I took away the crucial gem: Michael knew nothing of the upstream business and, having never been to Turkmenistan, he could not in any credible manner continue without me unless he was prepared to deliver himself and our future into the hands of Monument Oil. Shamefully, this was not the structure or shape of the management team conducive to getting the Game Plan done. Despite all, I also knew that I had to remain in contact and be present to catch the baby when or should my views come to pass.

Gladly, there was a silver lining (for as long as it may last) to the personal insult of Michael's actions: regular income. Not since May '93 had I received a regular income and through the consultancy of Balor, my personal company, to the overseas project of Turkmenistan, VSTT, a new capitalised company, would pay a retainer of £48,000.00 per annum based on my company being available to attend all pertinent activities in Turkmenistan and Russia on a 14 working day per month basis. This arrangement, in effect, gave me plenty of available time to attend to and prepare the Tacoma business plan of action along the West African margin, which I got into immediately.

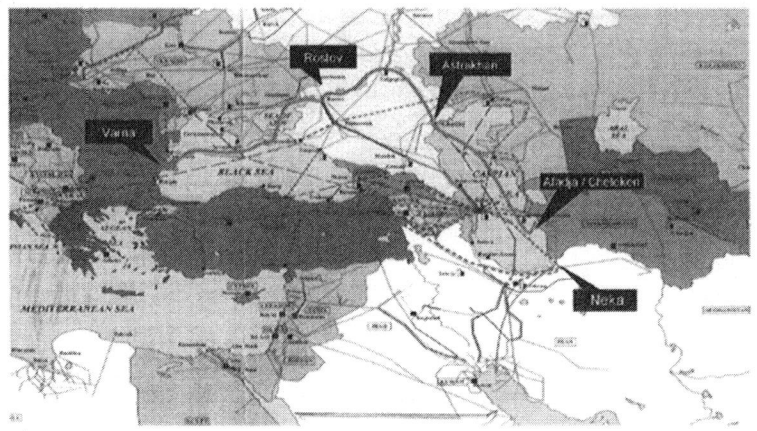

Burren Energy/VSTT first crude oil export rout to western market in 1995. Aladja, Cheleken to Varna, Bulgaria.

Architectural splendour of one lock gate on the Volga Don canal. Above: the first export route line in red from Cheleken to Varna.

Chapter 6
Into Africa

I spent time preparing for the business development trip to the various West African ministries that Andy wished would impress and improve his corporate standing. All the while, I was disappointed with Michael's decision and direction of focus. I could only assume that his partner Simon, a man whose mind, in my experience at least, was not altogether dissimilar from that of an elected Nigerian official, had intervened. I knew that the eventual business objective was still far off and was best achieved by the preservation of a cohesive team. Both Barings and Monument, for different reasons, would be greatly assisted in their commercial objectives by our divided management team, as the former had its financial teeth into Volgotanker and the latter was advanced in a new oil province for their own expansion. Michael, I assumed, would not agree with my view as he would not have been versed in the competitive style and approach of the hydrocarbon exploration and production upstream industry. He possibly assumed that the Bidding Agreement between Monument and VSTT was sufficient to both continue his stream of long lunch invitations with their legal and operations management team and guarantee his future of upstream wealth. Michael was experienced in streetwise business methods, especially with Simon as his Rottweiler driver; however, in my view, an upstream business development negotiation is a slow, long game best suited to a patient mind. A mindset embraced by Atul Gupta which, together with a cunning plan inspired from within the Monument Oil team, would cast STT adrift in the proceedings.

As I undertook the enforced time out from the daily activities of VSTT, and with a particular interest in maintaining a corporate presence within the Ashgabat community, I requested Sharif make visits to monitor the 'noise' in the corridors of the Ministry and Presidential office, which was starting to intensify as the Monument team got more comfortable with the contractual and technological negotiation proceedings. It was becoming clear to both Sharif and I that our past visits to earn our participation and future expectation of a beneficial partnership position were being diluted through the Monument presentation. While it remained imperative to have a western controlled export link to monetise the project, the link did have a shelf life as the region would become more interactive and collaborative between the neighbouring countries.

Nonetheless, my brother Adrian and I set off for our first destination as Tacoma's representatives to Abidjan in the Ivory Coast. I recognised and enjoyed the upgrade that the traders of the downstream sector could afford. The money, image and impression of 'being seen' was everything in this sphere, which juxtaposed sharply to the anonymous world I was more accustomed to of the explorer in the upstream.

I intended to present the image that Andy and Tacoma were committed and willing to undertake an upstream investment. Their team had proven corporate financial strength, technologically astute members along with both local environmental and community experience and wisdom.

However, I also believed that Andy was quite content that should an investment of this nature never occur, he would happily rest on a very spirited – if not feigned – approach that would count well with the refining and finance ministers of the respective countries visited. This approach suited me very well too, as the quote made by Michael but attributed to Monument over our recent meeting made clear: 'Finian is only a geologist and a not very good one at that.' This held some truth when considering in-depth sedimentary basin analysis required, as I was after all, a geophysicist.

****

I settled into the Air France drinks trolley and business class seat and began to think on my geophysical triumphs and failures. *The Geocor IV™1024 channel system had been developed during a period in the industry when a 24-channel system was routine and a 60-channel system a dream. The Geocor IV™ utilised '70s telecommunication technology from Caltech in Pasadena, developed to transmit data from the Voyager space mission vehicles into the 21st century known as Sign-bit Technology™. Geophysicalsystems Corporation was founded by two ex-United Geophysical engineers, Sam Allen and Link Martin, who took the patent and developed, amongst other accessory items, the Field Acquisition and Processing Geocor IV™ 1024 multi-channel system, which was a technological advancement at the time that improved the resolution and detail of the geophysical acoustic properties of the earth by 10-fold such that a high* resolution digital seismic acquisition system record could be acquired. Technology had shown through experience and academic study that an increase in the number of channels recording and stacking the same subsurface point would provide the geophysical interpreter a better view and with it increase the likelihood of identifying a feature or anomaly containing liquids, be that hydrocarbon or water. The Geocor was unique to the Australian exploration sector when I arrived as the country manager, aged 26, to undertake the company's first foreign seismic crew venture outside of continental USA. The company had sold a number of systems, but this was their first foreign operation. As I became familiar with the operations and the contracts for two field crews, I made numerous basic errors as a new and young manager, most notably I was too considerate to my crew personnel with preference for my popularity having failed to reduce the number of expatriate staff and their associated costs, despite training local personnel who proved to be better technically in the field and more adaptable to the hostile environment of the desert location. The local hirers were especially at home in our circus-lifestyle accommodation. To correct my ways, I learnt quickly to forget about the profit line and concentrate on cash as the timing of my entry into the market coincided with the first of numerous oil price shocks over that decade which scythed the number of operating onshore seismic crews across Australia from 32 on arrival to 3, eight years later when I had somehow still managed to maintain my two original, if battered, teams.

The parent company going into Chapter 11 bankruptcy didn't help but it did make me the only boss, as the banks in California needed my cash and I was too far away to catch. I side-stepped their bankruptcy and the technical limitations of costly external data processing through the geophysical capabilities of the same multichannel data which was available internally through a dedicated Geocor IV second unit and was designed to data process on site. I successfully marketed a stand-alone processing unit in-house alongside the excellent data that my teams and our technique acquired, the fruits of which would make my Australian operation debt free by May 1987 as well as continuously profitable thereafter.

I would reflect on my poor management and attempt to benefit from the coalface experience over those early years. I had reached a low point in the Australian winter of '84 with the near financial ruin of the company, when circumstances in the market deteriorated and I found that I was unable to manage the market correctly and generate free cash flow. The phone call from

Adrian coincident with these poor times was unfortunate, as there he was on the other side of the world seated in the parents' Rolls Royce during the twilight years of our father's good income after our mother's horse had won its maiden race, drunk on the delights of the moment. The thought to share it with me was generous on their part, but I found it difficult to rise to their joy being totally immersed and aware that my management had neither the money nor credit to pay the creditors or salaries later that month. Perhaps for the first time, but not the last, I was alone with my wife and children facing the whites of the creditors' eyes.

****

Sadly, the opportunities in both the Ivory Coast and Benin were all offshore. While the respective geology and petroleum systems were commercial for a major industry player, by my measure, they did not fit the fiscal and technological simplicity required to permit a Tacoma budget to satisfy the business purpose and risk. I did not wish to expose Andy to spending any serious money or losing company credibility in the process. Adrian and I both had to rely on our schoolboy French to engage and ascertain the value of the data provided. This proved challenging as we were both immersed in our respective efforts to speak Russian, which was already drawing on our limited linguistic reserves, and to add another tongue was beyond us. However, that didn't stop the revelries continuing at the lobby bar at the Hilton on the beach sitting alongside Satchmo the barman of 'that's my boys' fame'.

Over one technical review period in Benin, both Adrian and I had to copy, read and translate as much technical data as possible in the short time allowed and so I suggested that Adrian take the adjacent room to my poor ventilated, hot, sweaty and dusty one. While I concentrated on my work, there was a constant mumbling emanating from Adrian into the hand tape recorder along with much coughing and spluttering from the neighbouring room. Eventually, Adrian burst out of the room desperate for air – he had taken the adjacent room similar to mine but sadly included a well-used broken toilet!

Our reception in Congo Brazzaville was the most receptive of all, as Tacoma had much ongoing business. They enjoyed cargo lifting upwards of 40,000 tonnes per month of product and were constructing petrol stations accompanied with the western style shop. Congo Brazzaville was at that time our third country assignment following Benin and Ivory Coast. Adrian and I had by then perfected the Tacoma business presentation, probably aided by improved vocabulary and confidence through repetition, which got the desired and best result. Rather than being thrust cases full of offshore data bundles with vast risk attached, I got the opportunity that I was hoping for and was shown the data for a small onshore block recently relinquished by the French major, ELF.

There had been a discovery well with a modest resulting flow test that had been considered (learnt later by the ELF Paris office) not to be commercial. This was in my view the ideal and perfect project as it was onshore, marginal and obviously had a productive if not prolific reservoir. In my business view, Tacoma could receive plaudits for upstream investment without being dragged into a fiscal black hole of upstream expenditure. The appraisal and development-well budget required to make the small field commercial was negligible in comparison to offshore equivalent projects and, similar to all onshore marginal fields, the crude oil could be trucked to the nearest oil storage terminal and sold which, in this instance, was only 65km distance down the forested escarpment along dirt logging roads.

We departed Congo B' with a positive verbal report for Andy.

That evening's Air France flight showed more than the typical 'African' tiredness, as a crack in the third engine mounting was causing more than mere concern to the flight crew as they tried to casually walk past our window view of the lighted area. I was content with the trip and enjoyed the feeling that divergence away from the Game Plan gave me. I was not sure where the Tacoma plan would lead as it was still in my mind a business collaboration whose purpose was to support Tacoma's relationships and, therefore, may not move further than a goodwill performance.

Yet, I did feel that the Kouakuala Field or production licence area that we had reviewed had the perfect fit for a small, low risked investment for the business plan and my intended proposition to Andy on my return. Adrian had taken a cocktail or two in the front row of the business class section with a pair of Shell execs, as noted from their briefcase tags, who were only too glad to hear his story despite my semaphore actions from my rear seat while drifting off that he not do so.

****

I added the new countries to my still expanding list which then stood at 69. I thought of Australia, which counted as one, yet so huge and full of places such as Broome and Cable beach where I swam naked in '85 with John Dorrier of BHP, the largest of Australian mining concerns. We chatted on the incongruity of our situation and whether we would each meet again (only to meet up 20 years later when each a CEO and founder of our respective companies (Gulfsands and Burren)). The Washing Machine Corner, a so aptly named point in the Great Sandy Desert where a divide in the track led to Lon Loveless, the local party leader, to take one path in his unauthorised motor track bike and his assembled crew taking the other, correct route. He was found a few days later.

Then there's Glen Helen on the western end of the tarmac road out of Alice Springs, where the Afghan early traders and camels would congregate before making the next crossing over the deserts north or south at a time before the telegraph. Today, this is a wonderful water filled gorge and rough hotel run by a group of women. Rough Range on the west coast, perfectly named for its inhospitable access and terrain, was where our multichannel technology and technique revealed the hidden plays that explained the first onshore discovery in Australia in 1952. Those classic results led, in marketing terms, to our next year's contract and the move into Thailand a few years later.

Other interesting spots included Bauhinia Downs, the Northern Territory station hamlet and scene of the salty crocodile waddling down the street. The onward trek before reaching Mt Isa mine to drink in the largest Irish club bar in the world before crossing the Barclay flats into urban Queensland; Thargomindah, down from Quilpe in western Queensland, where one can enjoy the only dwarf throwing competition and back in North Western Australia to Fitzroy Crossing, noted from the first Space Shuttle commentary as being a vision of a 'crystal city' which, on official inspection, proved to be the sun's reflection off the largest tip of empty tinies of all time. Then there was the rare moment of mechanic humour on licence 175 of the Great Sandy Desert when the daily start crew routine was interrupted by a blast of white smoke exhaust from one of the four Vibrator truck units and, looking to Niven the mechanic, I observed that the Vatican announces a new Pope to the waiting public through the release of white smoke. To this, Niven replied, "If they have, can we get him here?"

The extraordinary moment just proximal to Uluru (Ayer's Rock) when I set off on the nine-hour drive back to Alice Springs or closer, should there be a road station, when the crew who were located so remotely and without any means of communication with the head office in Pasadena encountered technical problems with the software on the Geocor IV system. Not far from the camp, I stopped to chat with our line crew to explain the problem. Amongst the team was an aboriginal chap who told me that only a few miles along the track I would encounter a phone on a white table! I travelled those short miles to this solitary telephone and picked up the handle, got a dial tone and made the international call to California which led to resolution of the problem.

My closing comment over the call was describing the surreal location, standing as I was beside a gravestone facing a beautiful amber sun setting on the red landscape. A few days later, while getting petrol not far from Alice, I chatted with a local about the white table phone. "There was a white family," he told me, that owned the station and operated a motel with a pool. Sadly, their daughter died and was buried on the property. Later, the family were moved through a compulsory purchase agreement for Aboriginal land. Not pleased, the family bulldozed every building into the pool yet left a white table plus working phone on the side of their daughter's grave. The phone was paid for as part of the Aboriginal land settlement by the government.

I could see the beacons along the western horizon, perhaps the discovered gas flares from my time in Nigeria. An hour later over southern Algeria, I saw the flares of Hassid Masood, where I made the most ridiculous Geocor sales attempt, in French, to the NOC service company, only to spend the night amongst tribal Islamists plotting a coup as part of the imminent national rebellion.

I liked to remember both the reality and the humour of those days, especially my Australian ones. Those times created the founding experiences and gumption that provided the drive to get my Game Plan to work. I could hear that ubiquitous common shout 'give it a go ye mug', smiled and slept.

****

Back in the UK, it was high summer and time for a family holiday – a first since '92 – to a three-star package holiday in a Tunisian beach hotel. The team perfected the art of lunch making from their breakfast choice, evading the staff on exit with their heavy pockets. Amongst numerous family activities was the evening bilingual bingo where, thanks to the prevailing guest list being that of the UK holidaymaker with limited French, we were able to call the full card just in time to win enough money for a proper lunch the next day.

My return to the VSTT office coincided with the return of Michael after a long summer recess at his family base in Greece. I felt immediately the frost of the relationship with Michael and Simon, which became even cooler when my initial fears for the accountability of VSTT were realised on entering our basement domain: my solitary cost to Sumo had grown to include Charles and Sharif and a further five youths. In all, eight were part of the VSTT operation, an operation that had no business to tend to since the Vn220 lifting and re-introduction of the presidential embargo on crude exports. Personnel costs were being charged to VSTT accounts rather than allocated to the Sumo ship management operation, but then look who was counting.

Chapter 7
A Different Style

By summer '95, the rumours and facts continued to emanate from Ashgabat on a regular basis, which on each and every occasion brought more individual comment from the general Sumo shipping office community. VSTT had assumed an importance and a part to play in what was becoming, for the Sumo Shipping office, a real deal and, therefore, a potential source of revenue for all traders. The gathering crowd following each and every good lunch that Michael and Simon provided seemed to enlist yet more, who then came to my basement desk to tell me their part to play and how they had moved the project forward. I found silence to be the best strategy and form of defence and I kept my own counsel for exactly that purpose and plan.

The rumours from Ashgabat suggested that, on the one hand, the current oil export embargo would be lifted within the coming months, whilst other facts indicated that Monument was stuck in their negotiations. The impasse was created from their wish to introduce a format of an agreement drafted by the International Petroleum Association of the USA, an agreement better known as a Production Sharing Agreement (PSA). This style or format was used in almost all international regions where mineral and royalty rights were held by the government or crown and proportionally leased to a third investing party but was not understood, nor recognised, by the former Soviet law which at that time enshrined Turkmen law.

Monument's position and requirement for the PSA to be the accepted future agreement was a sticking – possibly breaking – point which I had to support given my earlier experience of the Turkmen contract. Only Sharif was up to date with the reality of crude oil exports, as he continued to acquire information sourced from his safe refuge within the Ashgabat community and the broader Russian river system network of port captains, repair yards and the numerous bunkering agents.

I reported our recent West African trip and business conclusion to Andy in his Geneva office. He was delighted with our progress as he took the proposal hook, line and sinker with tremendous enthusiasm; a response which was in direct contrast to his partner and fellow trader, Pierre Lasry. While I remained polite but aloof with Pierre, I recognised the distain that he felt for funds that could be better used capitalising trading positions than being tied up or wasted in an upstream project or fantasy. I didn't altogether disagree with him but was certainly not going to support such sentiment. Adrian had returned to Russia to function as Tacoma's new business development manager for European Russia, based in Volgograd. He played no further practical role in the Tacoma West African business plan which took on a new vigour and profile as Andy himself proposed that, between us, we would be able to elevate the 'work study' visits up to a project negotiation level.

The Game Plan became seemingly stuck in the molasses of Turkmen internal review, legal education or downright unwillingness to accept that a western agreement could be more beneficial to them than the former Soviet style. The two legal proposals rested on the point of defined responsibilities: a foreign contractor to be service supplier and remunerated accordingly on the Soviet style, while the western proposal elevated the parties to a partnership. Partners that would have clearly defined risk, fiscal and reward roles which, under western accounting standards and terminology, would permit the partners to have legal title over their proportional interest in the asset. This last and all-important point was the basis for crediting value against risk and reward, as the value of the asset or resource may then be booked or accounted through a technical or petro-physical computation and placed on a balance sheet. The African nations, most probably due to their legacy of colonial law, were well-adapted beneficiaries of the PSA law and had enshrined the law under their respective petroleum laws. Monument had an uphill task, but one that over the next six months or so they would accomplish.

Meanwhile, Andy and I departed for Brazzaville, Republic of Congo, or simply Brazzaville Congo, and a meeting with the finance minister. Such a meeting was a first for me as in the upstream exploration business the arrangement for introductory and customary visits to a new country would ordinarily be with the Ministry of Resources or equivalent. Meeting the finance minister was therefore extremely beneficial for the good reason that in Sub-Saharan countries the resource or energy minister usually had a political shelf-life counted in months, whilst the finance minister or vizier commonly held a personal or blood relationship with the ruling family that was measured in years or decades, dependent on the reign and level of corruption.

I had developed a theory, through my seismic interventions with African country officials, that the level and style of corruption within a political and administrative service, was dependant on the legacy of the colonial flag that ruled in the 19th and early 20th century. I noted that French past colonial legacy preyed on the developer through the ruling family and in particular, the wife or wives. An English past nurtured a corruption emanating predominately at the civil service level, German from the local authorities and finally Belgium, pure clinical corruption throughout and the worst case of the sad affair being the Democratic Republic of Congo or Kinshasa Congo. Brazzaville Congo's colonial past on the other side of the river, was under French administration.

It was always important that one never entered in at any level nor got drawn in through the early intervention of perceived 'lobbyist' types, as they had short fuses and shorter memories. The positive aspect of the hydrocarbon industry, especially upstream, was that the relationship would be expected to last numerous years, even decades. The very agreement itself gave the parties the opportunity to express their goodwill, efficiency and appreciation through legally binding appendices that addressed funding and which could and would be directed to spheres of work that directly or indirectly impacted on the contractual performance. Topics such as social housing, education, road building, health and numerous others could be addressed within the fiscal regime of a PSA, all of which would pass muster by an independent audit. The local distribution and management of funding to related topics would be addressed in the PSA and directed to pertinent chosen politically sensitive groups, which was in addition to the performance of individual actions both past and present in achieving the stated objective(s).

It was vital that Andy understood my view on this important matter as he, being an astute trading downstream player, would be expert in cultivating short-term relationship goodwill. This pragmatic cultivation of amity was no better exemplified than by his prudent application and interpretation of the draft wording within the product or crude purchase agreement (such as the date and formulae for price): the wording of the Letter of Credit is crucially important and can often determine the potency of a deal, such as the time that the funds remain as a credit and therefore accessible collateral to the Seller or an individual – hours, days or weeks – before transfer to the Seller's national bank account.

The working chemistry between Andy and I was received as a welcome surprise by the authorities, it having been many years since they had been confronted by the effective collaboration of experienced upstream and downstream teams working together. This was the obvious success of the union. Without the personality issues, the same could and must be said for the Sumo business relationship too. Both were unique in the latter part of the 20th century. The reception and level of the meeting with the finance minister was excellent in my view as Andy's perfect Swiss mannerisms, soft polite voice and fluent French worked its charm. A foul could have been directed against us by the energy ministry officials present, should they have reported back to their energy minister our 'rigged' relationship with the finance minister, as the former would no doubt be counting his lost reward for a project thoughtfully placed with his paying list of runners.

Following the daily round of discussions, our evenings were our own at the Hotel Meridien. On the first evening, Andy got a late-night call; when he finally appeared at breakfast, he announced our award of a 5% working interest in the offshore block Marine V, operated by Chevron. Impressive as this would be to the outside world, for Tacoma, it would be a disaster: the cost alone of a 5% contribution to Chevron's local overhead, proportional corporate head office administration and technical support (before any fixed capital expenditure) would put his company close to bankruptcy. I could not be more emphatic that he must decline the offer. He understood and responded the same back to the minister who I can only imagine must have been impressed as he called yet another meeting, but this time, a closed meeting. Andy, from my rehearsal, made the case for a small onshore interest, such as Kouakouala, which made the correct business impression and sense. If there was a need for a more impacting statement from Tacoma we would be willing to undertake, in addition, an exploration block and small work program commitment. A small work study committing us to geological and geophysical duties, as well as a report, before proposing or committing to seismic and drilling programs or, if not, then relinquishing our interest.

Leaving the minister to dwell on our proposition, Andy took off to his own company meetings with the planning team as he prepared to commence the building of his petrol station and shop, while I took a wander down to the right bank of the Congo River. I lay there and watched the rapids gather around the kariba weed that would stretch before it disintegrated while descending towards

81

the falls at Matadi. I was gifted with the sentiment of a passing gentleman with local experience and wisdom: 'if you lie there long enough, you will witness the body of your enemy float pass'. A truly wonderfully descriptive African statement and one that, for the first time, made me realise my proximity to the genocidal activities of the twentieth-century Belgian Congo. The contrasting view from my location was also an arresting thought: the mere two million seemingly content mass of Brazzaville humanity on the right bank across from, by only a mile or less, the 12+ million mass of deprivation living in the corrupt pyramid bubble that is Kinshasa. It would not be long before I and my Tacoma Resources team would be in a fast motor boat being driven between the towns as a mode of travel to reach meetings with respective ministry officials.

The morning of our departure arrived with the overnight decision (which again explained Andy's late calls and disappearances) that Tacoma would be invited to enter in a Memorandum of Understanding (MOU) for the onshore block Kouakouala and a yet to be defined exploration area which would ultimately lead to a PSA being signed within 12 months.

I headed home with a feeling of exhilaration having participated in the birth of another upstream project in a highly politically charged geographic location under the financial command of a businessman, less interested in his ego and image than his business approach and the prospect of economic growth in that country.

I reflected on the two contrasting parties with whom I was entangled, Michael and Simon on the one hand and Andy Dossenbach on the other, their divergence of their styles and personalities. I could envisage an alignment of their respective expectations and end game which, in an ideal world, should be a single technical team under one corporate roof.

****

Such a dream seamlessly faded into my children's births and surrounding idiosyncratic moments that happened at the King Edward hospital in Perth all those years ago. Milly born on 21 July '82 with my very limited part played out only when the telephone receiver above Di's head was answered by the attending nurse and given to me to answer. A radio phone-call from one of the crews in the Great Sandy Desert. Seemingly, a crew strike had ensued due to militant labour agitators but, amusingly, was given full management attention due to the one-way phone selection and call. All was proceeding in a crazy manner as their leader presented their views and demands over the one-way phone. During my response, there was a genuine birthing moment, commotion and concern in my voice that was heard by the strike leader, who then promptly enquired about the circumstances in which I was taking the call. I explained my situation and the militant leader graciously dropped all concerns for strike action and expressed amazement that I had taken the call.

In May '84, Diana was close to term in her next pregnancy but reassured me it would likely be a couple more days, so I drove north to join the crew out of Exmouth, WA. Road stations along the west coast are determined by pit stop fuelling distances approximately every six hours driving. I had reached the first when a message, passed on by the bush telegraph, told me to return as Di had gone into labour, having driven Milly to a neighbour and herself to hospital. I arrived much later only to fall asleep beneath her bed above which, Tessa soon arrived into peaceful surroundings. In what seemed a short time, Sophie then appeared in November '86. Within an hour of her birth, a speaker message was broad cast around the hospital for 'Mr O'Sullivan to go immediately to the paediatrics department'. Concerned, I went. On arrival, I was swept into the inner sanctuary to the head of paediatrics, a Dr Fred Grough. I had to prepare and fear for the worst, so was pleasantly surprised when I realised his request was for my professional advice! He was required to sign a seismic acquisition contract, to meet a midday deadline customs & revenue requirement over an exploration block that he and number of his colleagues had undertaken for tax purposes. I obliged him, there and then, with a few A4 sheets of contractual verse and a fix price of A$186,000.00 or A$2,480 per line kilometre acquired and processed up to a total 75 kms in his WA 176 block, which was conveniently adjacent to our proposed crew activity the following year, and achievable in a ten-day period.

****

That October, the Ashgabat rumour mill finally produced a useful fact: the embargo was to be lifted the following month and crude export lifts could once again commence. This time, the Volgotanker newswire corroborated it, which gave credence and clarity to the notice and once again set the financial letters of credit paper chain system printing. I was delighted, but given my 'consultancy' status would look on and observe while I waited for my chance to get involved.

Andy Dossenbach, Tacoma Resources & Trading.

Chapter 8
Into the Cold Chill

In addition to the five below stairs, there then appeared a sixth: a rather opinionated Icelandic chap who had clearly been the recipient of a good lunch by Simon. He immediately assumed operations controller status and therefore felt the need to give me yet another belittling speech on my having no part to play. I had satisfied myself that this chap, along with the others, except for Sharif, were expendable as they could not even point to the location of Turkmenistan or the Canal system on a map. A change from the earlier voyage charter agreement and programme with Volgotanker required VSTT to sign the ubiquitous Shell IV Time Charter Agreement. This style of operations would require very effective and experienced operators to ensure that the voyage time was conducted within cost. This I knew was going to be very demanding and full of pitfalls and potholes which required reliable 'local knowledge'.

Each of the four vessels chartered were called and presented Notice of Readiness or NOR, as requested and in good order, yet the Larmag loaded volumes having again been limited on the captain's preference were proving commercially unviable. Both Sharif and I, jointly and severally, had made visits to be present at each lift; over the course of the sixth lift, we managed to influence, or gain the respect of, the captains. From that point on, we saw the cargo capacity rise to economic levels above 4700 tonnes. Sharif's knowledge and diary of his supercargo trip from the previous year proved invaluable as specific lock-gate charges and delays also became an economic issue requiring our access to and influence within the local system, which was admirably undertaken and resolved by Anya Nikitina from Adrian's Tacoma Volgograd office.

Following each and every visit that I made to the loading terminal and vessel, I would 'disappear' away into the oil field regions towards Nebit Dag and wander over what would possibly soon be the first Turkmen PSA Agreement. The contract discussion between the Monument team and Turkmeneft was progressing as they, having taken foreign advice, took a positive view on the benefits the proposed fiscal regime a PSA generated for the host government in a royalty and production sharing arrangement.

The area had been delineated, as Arazov had correctly proposed over twelve months earlier, to enclose the known proven producing horizons of the Burun Field down to its known economic basement and a potential resource-surrounding fairway. The field was then producing approximately 9000 BOPD and decreasing, due to lack of investment and a sustainable daily maintenance operation. Walking over the field and surrounds, as I did on numerous occasions, was like walking through the film set of a Mad Max movie. The sheer dereliction and extent of waste of metals, materials, ground contamination, ruined shelters and office and maintenance garage facilities was a view of devastation. Away from the field and close to the Caspian Sea, but always visible from any point on the horizon, was the constant black smoke plume generated from the only gas exchange ionisation plant that produced photocopier black ink in the northern hemisphere. This was yet another surreal location: one where nature blends into a manmade furnace.

When back in the VSTT London office, I continued to remain silent on all rumours or facts of the upstream development, as good news would be broadcast either around the city restaurants and bars where competition would benefit, or around the office, where only more 'founding partners' would emerge. I applied the Logie Baird approach and responded to any pertinent question or discussion with a six-month virtual delay of old truths. The VSTT office numbers had swollen again with the addition of a bookkeeper from the Sumo Group. While a necessary position, it was not necessarily a position to be managed by a Sumo employee, particularly who so boldly managed the books in a prejudicial manner.

As the New Year came and went, I was ever increasingly concerned about the company's cash position. The transportation company was generating operating profits but was not conserving cash, as the cash movement through the Sumo Group was very dilutive. I felt beholden to remind Richard at Barings Asset Management of my concerns, as it would be simply ridiculous should the situation arise that the company – whose very existence in my and other stakeholders' view was to be a signature to a beneficial interest in an upstream oil and gas project – be then not able to do so due to bankruptcy proceedings or worse – a diminutive legal state that would be chanced upon by Monument to grab the whole beneficial interest whilst positioning VSTT as the sole nominated shipping company under revised terms. It did not bear thinking about but it did need addressing, which I did with Richard.

Over the midwinter months, voyage discharge ports and destinations altered to conform to the seasonal closure of the Volga-Don canal. All vessels were sub demised to Urals Trading and confined to the Baltic-Russian river system under Andrey's Urals Trading business model. The alteration effectively ceased crude shipment sales to Tacoma which, despite a reduction in revenue, maintained VSTT with a monthly charter revenue being the operator and transport agent. The imposition of yet another crude oil export embargo by the Turkmen President early in the New Year forced the transportation business into transporting petroleum products. The new style of business introduced the company to a new learning experience and commercial geography, which comprised making dedicated product liftings and transportation for Urals Trading at the refinery jetties of Turkmenbashi (aka Krasnovosk), Aktau and Ataray on the Kazakhstan Caspian coastline to discharge at railheads or other refinery jetties along the Russian River system. Whilst not generating revenue as before, it did give the operation a rewarding period of exposure to the 'real' world of Russian river shipping that would benefit the group, and especially Sharif, for future business ventures.

The convergence of the rumours from Turkmenistan and a breakdown in relations between Richard and Michael over the exceedingly poor cash position of VSTT was the backdrop to a wintery flight of the stakeholders to Ashgabat and a meeting with the energy minister – Essenov. The latter evolving from a rumour to a fact through a well-timed conversation between Brian and myself, confirmed over his last visit to Ashgabat, that the Monument negotiations were moving fast toward an agreement and the former being the worst kept secret on Folgate Street: the frustration of the fiscal and personal management of the company.

Through my personal contact with the office of Arazov, together with Sharif's supporting links, a meeting between the stakeholders of VSTT and the energy ministry was arranged with the express purpose of presenting the face of VSTT to the ministry: a meeting that would hopefully explain our 'silence' and non-participation in the negotiation thus far as well as our role in the partnership's future alongside Monument Oil.

The stakeholders gathered at Vnukovo airport, south of Moscow, and together flew on a Yak 40 private jet chartered by Urals, first to Samara,

Volgotanker's corporate head office, to collect President Strokin, and then onto Ashgabat. The plane was very slow and left much time to discuss strategy, which was something I guessed would be necessary when dealing with Volgotanker's President Strokin as he would never have considered going to Turkmenistan and especially not as an advocate for an upstream oil project or part investor in that country. As on recent meetings between Strokin and I, he had started to animate in English: when the topic came to the Game Plan and Turkmenistan, "Ooooo'Sullivan what have you done to me?" He was correct too, as it was because of him that the ministry and the minister were prepared to make the meeting, given the high respect still enshrined amongst authorities in Turkmenistan to 'foreign' officials from the Soviet times.

The ministry meeting started with Michael, with Andrey acting initially as an interpreter, making his usual effort to be the life and soul of the meeting with opening comments that would normally bring a smile or more in London, but here fell on the deafest ears as this meeting was colourless and would remain so. It was vital that the meeting was conducted in Russian, which was not a problem as three fifths of the stakeholders present spoke Russian, leaving Michael and I as observers. Both Andrey and Richard took control of the meeting, as I hoped they would, and presented the official picture inclusive of our expectations which, I could see by the body language, were not what Essenov was anticipating. Without a question of doubt, Brian and the rumours had been correct all along. Monument had not just written VSTT out of the script, they had never introduced us. Fortuitously, Andrey's vast espionage experience and Richard's natural tenacity and charm created the image of unquestionable support for the process, availability of a dedicated transportation network to the country and, through Richard's corporate name, willingness to invest in the future progress of the country. While Strokin continued to sit in silence like an emperor, our corporate persona was fixed and on departure would remain a virtual fresco on the wall, despite Essenov never once breaking his unwelcoming Soviet demeanour. I knew that Essenov didn't care for me, any more than he did in those Aziz days, but I also knew that that was history, history which had been trumped by the commanding performance of Andrey and Richard in his office that day.

It was on the return leg to Samara that the shape of the company altered, with the customary aggression. Each stakeholder, other than Michael, realised the implication of the meeting as we each concluded that what had seemed one man's dream a mere 24 months earlier was actually very close to reality. Both Andrey and Strokin knew from the Soviet style and message in the meeting that a deal was being done and that 'whilst your company name was absent over the course of negotiation we, the Ministry of Energy, do understand that you are part of the deal'.

Richard knew that the company was on the verge of a sensational valuation upgrade and financial correction. However, Michael, not well versed in being side-lined in meetings, seemed to have missed the message of the meeting and insisted on promoting his ship management appeal to Strokin over the course of the return flight. I could see the division in the conversations as drink found the spot and the direction of the discussions moved toward the topic of current management.

On Strokin's departure at Samara, the plane stood parked to refuel on the tarmac in a remote location and surrounded by military as foreigners who did not have permission to disembark were on board. How the level of discussion and venom rose so fast I was not quite sure, but before I was even aware of the chill rushing through the open door, Andrey had taken Michael from the aeroplane and out onto the tarmac without a coat. I could see through the window as Andrey proceeded to round on Michael with a withering tirade. Michael was clearly defenceless, surrounded, as they were, by military men that Andrey would casually embrace to signify which side they were on. Following a lengthy period of time and with poor Michael close to frozen, he was brought back inside the plane and left to himself. Further into the flight, I was taken aside by Richard and Andrey to be offered the position of Managing Director of VSTT, which I duly accepted. In my view that was always my position, but I had kept that thought silent too. I felt for Michael, but then, as throughout, was not the moment for sentimentality given the demands of the business road ahead. Michael would not forget this event and would play the injured and aggrieved party thereon and through to the end as these events would herald the end of Michael's management participation in VSTT. The change also brought a noticeable shift in his attitude to the venture as a whole as his demeanour began to embrace the glass half empty view that, in my opinion, sadly determined the extent of the dilution of his and Simon's just and due reward for the Game Plan itself.

On my return to London, I set about doing what I knew best to do under the circumstances: engage the well tested seismic cash management style along with a move from the Sumo group office. Sharif found the perfect spot off Lincolns

Inn Field, which we opened for business in the spring of '96 with five staff, inclusive of a new accountant from the major BG group and Stephanos, the classic Greek expense-account driven trader who had developed a working relationship with a young rising star from Glencore, Kirk Lazarus. I took advantage of this relationship as well as my own with Strokin by adapting to the seasonal changes in the Russian River shipping calendar and replacing the cash-draining time charters with Caspian Sea dedicated voyage charter agreements for vessels on a continuous basis. Within months of commencing operations under my management, the company was on a cash positive basis and maintaining 'radio' silence over the rumour mill coming out of Turkmenistan. Our new image became the company to talk with for all new Caspian players requiring transportation advice and discharge ports, which suited me perfectly as, with Redmayne before, I was just the ferryman generating revenue through employment of the fleet for Glencore and others as and when required. Most important of all, we were a company on a steady footing ready for the event in Turkmenistan to become reality.

(L-R) Diana, Milly, Sophie, Tess, myself and Vicki Polities
(one of Burren's traders) opening the new Lincoln's Inn field Office

Chapter 9
Rags to Riches

It was by then five years since leaving my last management position in Australia. Five years spent in a wilderness, collecting experiences for that virtual jigsaw puzzle, so that I might one day create again the picture that once reflected my life in Australia. The image was by no means near complete, indeed there were thousands of pieces yet to be found. However, I felt that I was on the clear and open road to finding those missing parts to make the landscape, as I was by then in control of my own destiny. Under my direction, I knew that, should the events in play conform to my expectations, then the picture puzzle could be made complete. The immediate objective was to ensure that VSTT was ready to perform at the point of a Monument Oil result. This was important as I knew that within the Monument team there would be issues, especially with alternate allegiances created by the recent changes at VSTT, and they would try to benefit from VSTT's confusion.

Maintaining fleet operations in the Caspian was the constant brief, with the requirement of having a presence on the ground to respond to any unusual behaviour of the port officials. Without notice, the port authorities would not allow a vessel to NOR (prepare to load), which required me or Sharif to entertain the usual austere inducement of 200 cigarettes or talcum powder, should the official be female, to either release the vessel or proceed with loading. On one occasion, circumstances led to the most comic moment where our company future cash flow depended on the release of a vessel. The very officious official insisted on a company stamp (which we did not have) for the discharge papers before releasing the vessel. I had Sharif take the official aside in conversation while I reached for any coin in my pocket and sealed the deal with the beautiful rouge stamp of the Queen's head on a Turkmen document. This was the first, last and only occasion, I believe, that a two-pence coin was used as a frank to seal an official Turkmen document.

Working with Glencore and Kirk illuminated the wonderful world that I came to understand as the archipelago of offshore banditry. Each Bill of Lading filed had a different purchasing company registered in a different part of the world. On one occasion, where they requested clarity of the buyer, the island and registry was changed along with the company name. The transportation business had moved on from the illustrious days with Andy and Tacoma, as they were converted and working towards an upstream objective, while my team at VSTT moved further downstream yet with a similar objective. The decision of which 'hat' to wear on my days in London was as random and frequent as the rain. Whether I was VSTT transportation midstream, a Sumo trader or exploration advisor to the upstream technical requirements for the collation of data from Congo to review and store, as per the limited budget, was wonderful whilst more pieces of the puzzle kept appearing.

When passing through Moscow, following visits to Turkmenistan, I continued to update Andrey and the ever more attentive Mike Calvey on the shipping and upstream developments. On one of the homebound flights, I had a chance meeting with a gentleman whom I had last played host to in Perth but had not followed up since my return to the UK, despite our neighbourly location in the Hampshire area. Lord Torrington, or Tim as I knew him, was not in a good way.

As people do when their very commercial existence seems threatened, they discuss their shortfalls with strangers rather than take the counsel of their loved ones. It somewhat amused me and simultaneously confirmed to me the attributes to my reclusive business style, when Tim told me of his business development venture in Turkmenistan. He believed that his endeavours were proceeding at a great pace toward an opportunity to render Monument Oil a blow. He had been under the belief that Heritage Oil and Gas were imminently about to step into the Monument negotiating seat, but his timing had been undermined and he was left returning to London and his board with poor news that could prove to be his last report. The story did not surprise me as I knew that there was competition, but from which company I knew not. However, I was aware that the competition was addressing the wrong court. Heritage Oil were following a political agenda that led them up and against the president's interest and authority. I remained impartial, neither confirming nor denying knowledge of these events, as that would have drawn out my participation. Given my and Tim's pleasant initial meeting many years earlier in Australia, I did however see an extremely interesting alternative opportunity. I remembered that Tim, despite his membership of the House of Lords, was an extremely diligent and well-travelled geologist within the African continent. I therefore took the remainder of the flight to relay to Tim the Tacoma activities and our position in the Brazzaville Congo.

Within a week of our return and following an introduction over the phone with Andy, the two parties – Heritage Oil and Tacoma Resources – signed a Mutual Bidding Agreement and Area of Mutual Interest Agreement for the Brazzaville Congo on terms that amounted to equal equity participation. To earn their participation, Heritage would match Tacoma's estimated cost to date through payment of the next contributory costs of the negotiation etc., up to $300,000.00. This arrangement for Andy, similar to that for Michael and Simon with both parties holding 50% respective carried interest, was an excellent outcome. The nature of both projects from conception through to development was similar, as both had upstream objectives with a real chance of reaching a PSA. Both were subject to political risk, but the climate in the West African region had the storm clouds building on the horizon as cross boundary tribal tensions rose.

As night follows day, we took our seat at the first partners meeting where Tacoma the founder partner, as VSTT was with Monument, were made to feel second-class citizens amongst the glorified upstream white-collar elite. This time, much to Tim's astonishment, I made it clear that we, Tacoma, respected and accepted the Heritage technical lead but when on site in Brazzaville Andy was to be the voice of reason with the government officials. This, Heritage accepted, mutely agreeing it was worth the disruption in relations. The working relationship between the parties thereon proved stable, which in the end made for a prosperous arrangement.

I returned to Turkmenistan to continue my visible presence on the ground amongst the Ashgabat officials, yet was diverted away into the reclusive pairing with Kirk, who had his own businessmen community by then. This community included the eccentric character Murad Babayev, a character out of the Arabian Nights replete with a cellar even Churchill would have admired, full as it was with the most exquisite Armenian brandy in frosted glass bottles. We found this nectar was best enjoyed between 7–11am along with strong coffee.

As the time of day moved through casual meals in Turkmen style on-floor rugs and pillow support, Kirk would acquire inventory of product cargo or even snake oil, which was all bought on the government regulated Ashgabat commodity exchange at Murad's command with a messenger or runner service. The inventory would grow, and with it my fleet engagement itinerary, unlike the meeting's atmosphere which became surreal and moved further towards the existential as time wore on. Our surroundings became positively theatrical when Kirk mentioned that it was O'Sullivan that had brought him Turkmenistan business. This fact created the most animated response from Murad, who immediately expressed a great desire to meet this man. He had heard both good and bad from the Ashgabat circus over time. Kirk most casually and reservedly mentioned to Murad that the very man he sought to meet was his guest right in front of him, lying on the floor. The noise levels rose with both his joy and my incredulity of all that was happening around me. On reflection, I pieced together the last 12 hours and concluded that, in the sequence of events, I had not been introduced to Murad other than by my Christian name, which of course in the eastern Slavic nomination of the family name first would have meant nothing to Murad in personal recognition or connection with any individual. The sequence of events moved from the existential to the ridiculous as Murad insisted that we all leave immediately for Nebit Dag, which we would reach by first light, to engage with Kulniazov, the new minister for the Balkanabad region and his close 'brother'. Murad was convinced he had the power to deliver not just any oil field, but the Kotor Tepe Oil field. I was quaking with thoughts of the potential merits of the plan to advance the status of VSTT but also the risk that it may corrupt our relationship with Monument as I knew that good relations at this very sensitive time were critical to the standing of VSTT, as rumours of an imminent signature to a PSA Agreement were rife in the resources community. In any event, it was the state of Murad's car that came to dictate our future.

Over the course of the first 20 miles, the fast and comfortable but less than well-maintained BMW 7 series lost one tyre to the pot-holed tarmac at speed, before losing a second not long before the 100-mile mark. The ridiculous became most serene as the three of us sat on the side of the road tired, sobering and silent except for Murad who serenaded us with Turkmen folk songs while the dawn broke on the eastern horizon. The light slowly exposed the apricot grove set out before the summer wetlands, where the bird life began a defence of their territory and retaliation to Murad's noise with their daily chorus. By early morning, we were back on the floor of his dining room, enjoying the biscuit sweet brandy and reminiscing on the pleasant drive to Ashgabat in the back of the watermelon seller's open truck. The oil field would have to wait for another day thought I, and it did.

As Kirk made local calls to arrange, or rather hitch, a lift from a passing business contact by taking a private plane from Ashgabat to Turkmenbashi early that afternoon, I saw that he was without a doubt a different business animal from any in my past. I joined him in a marketing meeting with a representative from the refinery but left early to have a swim in the Caspian Sea. It was more a necessary wash than a recreational activity. That evening, we both caught the local scheduled flight and some short sleep while crossing over to Baku. There, the meetings and activities continued in an even more ruinous state as clothes and accoutrements became long forsaken. Baku having not attained European status or the western building styles of the 21st century was rather bereft of water and had electricity shortages on a daily basis which affected most all the neighbourhoods. This, and the days on the move, had indeed played havoc with my attire and, in particular, my under attire, for the lack of water or paper prevented me from using my socks and underwear in the prescribed manner.

Using Kirk's expense account, we both returned to London via Frankfurt (which provided sanitary relief) before arriving early on the fifth morning to rest up on his floor until midmorning when a call reached me from Sharif, through Stephanos, to Kirk that alerted me to a meeting with Monument Oil, arranged at no notice but a must-be-there event! Without socks or underwear and still with stomach issues, I made my departure from Kirk's company back into the upstream white-collar world, but without the white collar.

Approaching, I noticed the meeting place was not at their office but rather in an administrative building of no consequence. In the reception, I caught up with Richard, Michael and to my disappointment, Simon. As each was ignorant of the topic or matter of business there was a quiet curiosity to our collective manner as we were shown into a boardroom where, in addition to the three Monument men including Tony that were well known especially to Michael and Simon, we were confronted with two unknown gentlemen, one of whom was an American. The pleasantries were normal with Michael, as ever, attempting to manoeuvre his standing with high-level business small talk while Richard and I took in their body language, which was not giving much away. An agenda followed the pronouncements made by Tony that present were representatives of Monument Oil, the signature party to the Burun Field PSA, VSTT, a transportation company and representatives from Mobil Oil!

After a moment of air sucking from the VSTT party, the meeting moved quickly through their agenda to the business of negotiating a Joint Participation

Agreement and the all-important Joint Operating Agreement (JOA). The former legally bound the investing parties together with their participation or equity interest illustrated, and the latter dictated which of the partners would lead all aspects of the field and administrative operation being nominated as the operator. The remaining parties, or non-operating parties, held proportional voting rights to capital expenditure, accounting, liabilities and, more collectively, cementing the rights and procedures for the contractor to perform under the terms of the PSA.

This all came as a bit of a shock to the VSTT team, given the circumstances, and even more so as the chemistry presented by the Mobil team to VSTT seemed rather hostile and echoed by Monument. The agenda was directing the view that VSTT was an irritant to this party – a potentially troublesome group that could and should be kept out or, at best, in their place.

To me, still cramped by the stomach pains, this was the concluding act of Monument's long running show since early 1995 of shadow-casting VSTT as anonymous. The Mobil attitude seemed in agreement but, to me, their attitude seemed wrong and out of place for American etiquette, especially as we had only been introduced. Their knowledge of us seemed spoiled or spiked, as they viewed us as a tyrannical partner that was or could be an embarrassment and, as such, should be treated with contempt.

I took regular departures from the room due to my stomach condition which was noted by the key Mobil negotiator and token American – Bob Parker. Sensing a clandestine act associated with each of my departures, he followed and confronted me on my third or fourth return along the adjoining corridor. I explained the events of the past five days, my stomach condition, my lack of socks etc. as well as my shoddy dress but, more importantly, I took the opportunity to brief Bob as to who and what part VSTT had played in the project to date. Like vodka splashed onto a frosted windscreen, Bob immediately saw through the propaganda and together we returned to the meeting room whereupon Mobil became the noblest supporter of VSTT.

Chapter 10
Off to Dallas

From the first trip to Turkmenistan three and a half years earlier, the Game Plan had been realised with little or no capital inflow. That is, if one could distinguish between Michael and Simon's ship management costs and pure VSTT expenditure. I sat alone to consider the sequence of events and the evolution of the result since walking out of the meeting with Roger and the TYT Turkish bank group at the Independent Hotel. The analogy of the lad on the Orinoco River gathering momentum from the minor tributary to join the fast-flowing river where sand bars, currents, flesh-eating fish and tidal wash would have to be overcome before reaching the high sea seemed to fit my situation. I enjoyed the 'westward ho' schoolboy imagery but knew that, far from the boys-own features, the reality required my continued vigilance of cash management and no amount of self or side-line adulation would deflect me from that duty.

I had by then spent thirteen years of my career, including Australia, managing cash and people. I had arrived at the pinnacle with a participation in an oil and gas production project: a valued core asset with primary production, where all horizons were subject to nature's reservoir performance and the value down to man's crude oil price. These results and values would emerge to be my master, dictating the time when very large sums of capital would be required from VSTT to meet our proportional interest of the cost of the Joint Operating Agreement (JOA).

VSTT signed the JOA with a beneficial working interest equity holding of 25% in the Burun PSA. The company had 'sold' down to Mobil from their initial holding of 50% for a cash-and-loan carry over a period of JOA expenditure up to $15million. Under this agreement, VSTT would not be required to fund its participating interest for an estimated period of two years from the Effective Date of 1st February 1997. Over that two-year period, it was expected that the project would have achieved positive cash flow. This was the expectation and one that most all would accept as credible given the terms of the PSA, the operating standards of the partners, the petroleum system and the all-important current and forecast price of a barrel of crude, which at the time of signing the agreement was $23.50 per barrel of Brent.

Between signing the PSA in August and the Effective Date on 1st February 1997, the date when we, the foreign contractor, took contractual control of all the financial, technical, environmental and human resource components of the field, was a phoney time. The two recognised parties got behind closed doors and smart dinner tables, without the inclusion of VSTT, as they didn't expect to hear from VSTT until money was required, or a ship, or both, depending on whichever arose first. For our part, I was quite understanding of that lack of recognition and was therefore quite surprised to get an invitation to Dallas and be fussed over by their Central Asian group who were charmed at meeting a genuine midstream shipping personnel that oddly seemed to have a good, if not advanced, knowledge of 3D seismic, drilling, geology and geophysics and could talk Caspian transportation over a beer.

Away from Mobil's generous invitation, I could feel the growing pains of the company or, more, the change in direction that the PSA signing had on the trading team, in particular Stephanos and his wonderful friend Vicki. Their departure made room and cash available to shore up the shipping operations with the arrival of the technical ship manager from the Sumo Group – John Stanton, a good man that I had learnt to respect from my time sitting amongst his team in the basement of Sumo's Folgate Street office building. Alongside Sharif, John brought vast international experience in all aspects of shipping, which broadened our little shipping group's ability to respond and secure Glencore trades. Quite out of the blue, yet perfect timing for VSTT's new status, Brian left Monument. This was partly because their corporate philosophy moved away from that of an entrepreneurial business development style which focused on exploration to that of an oil field operator style, but mainly so that he might follow his own entrepreneurial interests and set up his own company, Beacon Energy.

Brian was extremely willing to supplement his income as a consultant to VSTT by becoming our upstream technical and JOA representative at the management meetings, which was a huge benefit to me as I had experience neither in the strict authoritarian management of a JOA nor the formality of the calendar meetings. The arrival of Brian could not have been more helpful to the future tasks ahead as I would be required to conduct yet another legal corporate review, which precipitated yet more contentious, fractious and ugly spats with Michael and Simon. This was all happening whilst I was simultaneously attempting to glue together another shareholders agreement to address, amongst other issues, our future fund-raising requirements. It was going to be a long and dirty road to cut the rough VSTT stone into the beautifully clear, transparent and multi-faceted lustre of the sort of diamond our current asset demanded. This objective would become the next major milestone over the coming year.

The company housekeeping continued with the opening of a representative office in Ashgabat. Sharif took his unique style of the quiet achiever to the task in hand, which included the purchase and mobilisation of a new 4x4 for our office and a new bed for Anna as recompense for her kind help over the years. Further, he hired Sapar Dordeve, Anna's much younger partner, as the company driver who had a personality in keeping with his driving – one that could not get into sixth gear.

Andrey, who since the signing of the JOA had become much more conversant, helpful and useful in all areas, chose our Turkmen general representative and trader, (another) Sapar, who would prove useful for information collection given his past, like Andrey's, in the KGB.

****

I was on the Amoco contract crew in March '86 in the Northern Territories of Australia, when the call came from their operations office in Houston to demobilise the crew and quit the area. They had chosen to deploy their option to terminate the contract as it had been overrunning for more than three months pending the weather window, which was forecast to close. In fact, I had been extremely fortunate as both crews had made excellent free cash, possibly even a corporate profit, against previous year losses. However, the free cash had been repatriated to the parent company in California in order to maintain their bankruptcy status. In retrospect, there may have been a more sinister reason for the termination as within one month of that date the crude oil price fell dramatically and, with it, all hope of a new contract for the foreseeable future. It was lock down time, termination time and stack-the-crew equipment time, except for a smart move to locate both recording units to the car park of the Western Mining Corporation's Adelaide office and earn monthly processing revenue. For the rest, it was shut down.

As the Australian onshore hydrocarbon exploration market closed, I adopted the accounts standard of not paying until you can see the whites of their eyes. I had to beg time and perform acts of contrition to protect our very existence with delayed and very late payments, while at the same time address the market. The only onshore exploitative market alive was the gold and metal sectors. I, along with my protégée, Steve Tobin, took to the streets of the minerals community, a more geophysically adept and academic community that was able to promote a customised technical use of our unique equipment. We professed to being able to identify the extreme shallow lithology where commercial mining interest lay. Our very survival opened a new opportunity in an experienced sector which gave us financial breathing space with small, lucrative contracts which would maintain one crew, equipment and staff on roll-over term contracts. Like gypsies, we moved between the crew equipment stacked in the Western Australian Desert to work for CRA and the equipment in the western Queensland to work for BHP Minerals.

By May '87, the company had paid off its creditors including the First Boston long-term debt and, equally important, had produced some stunning geophysical results from both the mining and re-emerging hydrocarbon sectors. The results not only generated work but also broke the curse of the Shell Corporation, as they had an international ban on the Geophysical systems technique. Through my teams work for Ampol Exploration in the Rough Range area of WA, we had been awarded a West Australian Petroleum Exploration Pty Ltd (aka Wapet made up through 2/7 Shell, Texaco and Chevron Corporations and 1/7 Ampol Exploration) contract for a 3-dimensional survey, a first over their producing facilities on Barrow Island, Western Australia. This was a wonderful moment, but one that introduced a difficult matter of a human resource nature: Barrow Island operations was a male-only preserve. I had been the first to introduce women into remote seismic operations in Australia. In my view, their presence improved the male hygiene, language and work ethic while they worked earnestly up to an atmospheric tipping point when, if more than eight women per crew of 24, they would start to argue amongst themselves resulting in the male component becoming demoralised. This was especially true for the older men on the team, as it stressed their father figure characteristics. My human resources experience ran too: all field mechanics were drunks, cooks were homosexuals, surveyor's serial polygamists and female vibrator driver-operators lesbian, but then I was not an institutional industrial science driven manager.

On the back of the geophysical results from this period, Steve and I took to the geophysical seminars in Australia, US and Europe to proselytise the technique and success of the methods which brought not only contracts for ourselves but also equipment sales for the US corporation to India and China, and would lead to the mobilisation of one crew from Australia to Thailand. Supported by our success and the parent company's ability to survive through their renewed equipment sales and domestic academic survey work, I made overtures to Sam and Link (and through them to the Californian banks) to acquire the Australian company. I had financial support from local Perth based entrepreneurs plus institutional support from Tony Treadgold amongst others. If successful in my acquisition, the company would become the first Australian flag flying seismic company which, we believed, would guarantee local contracts before foreign contractors. Sadly, the US decision makers were not favourably disposed to the idea as they explained that our team's work was their cash from the golden cow. This was a disappointment and one that would lead, over the next two-year period, to my making plans to leave. For Steve, it would prove to be the making of his fortune as he enacted the same business plan over the following five years after my departure.

Chapter 11
Expand Where You Can

The vacuum created by the instant exchange of atmospheric pressure which occurs when an individual dream becomes a corporate reality was the medium that allowed the metamorphosis of the VSTT board to evolve from that of the Neolithic warrior class into a credible democratic blend of financial and industry individuals, each with expansive entrepreneurial spirits.

However, before that final board structure would be realised, Richard, who was both the Baring Asset Management director on the board and the only institutional investor representative, felt that his participation contravened the growing US sanctions foreign policy: as a US citizen, he was participating in business directives that could be interpreted as beneficial to the Islamic Republic of Iran. This was undeniable and, in the estimation of the board, was a fact that was only going to grow as, in keeping with Larmag, we intended to benefit from crude oil exchanged between the load port at Cheleken on the Turkmen Caspian coast and discharged, using our vessels, at the port of Neka on the coast of north Iran. Given a following wind of rising crude prices, the exchange deal was unbeatable, as the producer received international Arabian Gulf spot prices supported by improved quality figures. The board could predict with confidence that the fleet would support business development with Iran, which of course it did, and in time went further to the point of joint venture with Navion, a Norwegian based company with technical discussions directed at creating a Caspian class new design and built vessel. However, and with regret, the board lost Richard, a good institutional and individual player.

Mike Calvey, also a US citizen and once a partner of Richard's, seemed less concerned for his US status given his permanent domicile in Moscow. Since the early days of '94, he unceremoniously joined and expanded a private equity branch with interests transferred from the Baring Asset Management groups into a private concern. The emergent group, Baring Vostok Capital Partners, dedicated to Former Soviet Union investment alone, held a portfolio of investments inclusive of VSTT. The management, based entirely in Moscow and without representation in London, took over the management and board position in VSTT and further strengthened its equity holding in VSTT through the acquisition of Volgotanker held equity in VSTT in exchange for Barings debt due from Volgotanker.

I could understand the mentalities at play with President Strokin's mindset as he was never a genuine supporter of the Game Plan. Strokin's only interest, and correctly so, was to acquire financial support for his ageing fleet, which he had successfully done at the initiation of VSTT. As such, he was able to reduce that debt burden through exchange of Volgotanker equity in VSTT. In a parallel universe and without my knowledge, Michael and Simon of Sumo Group had undertaken a similar arrangement with their strong patron and worldly shipping magnate, Chios Energy (the Tsakos family group through one of their family holding companies). Andrey at Urals Partners had also taken this moment in the evolving business plan to exchange interests with his long-time and ageing partner, such that he, Andrey, retained sole interest in VSTT through Sunfloat Trading. The corporate list on the VSTT board and shareholder was thus complete with Sunfloat Trading (Andrey Pannikov), Chios Energy (Tsakos family), Sumo (Michael and Simon), BVCP (Mike Calvey), Volgotanker (President Strokin) and myself (Balor Holdings).

The new individual to appear on the scene, and one that came to assist the Barings camp as an alternate board director for Mike being as he was permanently based in London, was Alastair Stobie. Alastair, a 27-year-old UK citizen and wonderfully fun lad, had been recently let out from the army and was looking for more adventure. I was delighted to embrace him as the new arrival as he came dedicated to the show, owned a proper suit and tie, had the credentials for the growing requirement of 'city & board' and, equally important, could act as an impervious wall for the deteriorating relations between Michael, Simon and I. The executive benefits of this new addition and organisational structure were immediately apparent to me and all the more so to the company accounts, as the changes came extremely cheap given that they were all attained through (an act later to be named by Andy) the 'Burren Bonus' – a beer and a hand shake.

There were immediate opportunities to embrace fresh business ventures with this newfound team of highly motivated players. The party, including Sharif, agreed to gather in Ashgabat for a meeting with Murad Babayev and the chief minister for the Balkanabad region – Kulniazov. There was no need for the tiring trip in the BMW only to lose more tread or hear more of Murad's folk repertoire as, this time, the Mountain had come to Mohammad. Over a couple of sessions where the characters exchanged valued knowledge both of the regions and their stories, a simple Area of Mutual Interest Agreement (AMI) was signed between the regional minister and VSTT to include none other than Aziz, the Kotor Tepe oil and gas field. The opportunity cost of $100,000.00 to achieve the agreement was high given what followed. As we sealed a simple document, a grand announcement was made from the president's palace and the energy ministry for a similar AMI Agreement but, unlike ours, it was inclusive of the vast western region, excluded the offshore and onshore Burun field, and was signed by the government and its joint partners Mobil and Monument (without VSTT). Without doubt, this document carried all the gravitas required in the country to achieve its goal and trumped our AMI in the process. It was totally coincidental in timing that both parties had taken similar action, without notification, and explained why VSTT had not been invited to join the senior team as we had played our 'shipping' ace, won a hand but not the rubber.

Slightly aggrieved but not in despair, I would take the view that our document could act as a 'spoiling document-in-waiting' which, if taken to an international tribunal, could be the basis to plead foul play and thereby induce the senior party to offer terms of inclusion to VSTT rather than prolong legal recourse. I knew it was weak, but then, my recent understanding of 'pre-emption rights' from the JOA legal document had a connotation which, if used in a hostile manner, could be viewed similarly.

The opportunity to gather in Turkmenistan with Andrey, Sapar, Alistair, Sharif and myself was invaluable, as it harnessed the excitement and encouragement that flowed from the deal with Mobil and Monument. Both corporate bodies were present in Ashgabat setting up their respective operational offices which was wonderful for me to witness as I remembered my first visit nearly four years earlier. The success of the AMI in Turkmenistan, through our local contact base and technical knowledge, led seamlessly to a similar business potential that Andrey, with the technical support of VSTT, could repeat within his contact base along the numerous Southern Volga River Oblast regional authorities. Once again, the business approach that had proven successful with Tacoma in West Africa with the upstream and downstream teams working in unison, could be presented with Urals or Andrey as the trader. However, there was one fundamental obstacle: that an operating foreign owned or foreign majority held Russian company could not be a beneficial owner of resources in

Russia due to the lack of foreign ownership of legal title under the Russian petroleum law (or Property Law in general) for crude, both above and below the surface. This was simply down to the Soviet property laws which stipulated that only the state, or a state-owned organisation, could own title. This was understood and would be addressed following consideration and given due commercial and legal process.

I had learnt that there was a weekly 'milk' run flight from Ashgabat via all major port locations up the Caspian and Volga River to Samara, including Volgograd, where Adrian was based and a seat available on the next flight. In the vintage prop plane, the Antonov made the gradual climb out and along the Kopet Dag mountain chain that borders Iran before turning north-west over the Karakoram desert toward Aktau. Basic as a Soviet seat maybe it was always comfortable, which allowed me to doze…

****

The noise and low flight levels confirmed that the door was not closed, but since few seemed to care it was taken as normal for an '89 daily Bangkok to Rangoon service. I took up the invitation from the BHP Petroleum, changed recently from Hematite Petroleum, to respond to a bid invitation and scout their new foreign acreage. Their previous invitation to tender and scout in Assam had been more a good-will exercise, which was rewarded with a lengthy contract in the Sandy Desert but not in Assam, as terrain and access were prohibitive to a truck-mounted crew. Their Burma acreage was simpler and more accessible, but suffered as a country destination for western business.

I had perfected my taxi formulaic third world business routine: On arrival at the airport taxi rank would the driver put on the counter? If not, then soft currency and weak imports. Would the driver stop for a red light? No, then no rule of law, police corruption or usually both. Are the children playing and smiling on the streets? If not, then a corrupt dictator in power providing minimum or no labour regulations, or no freedom of speech. Burma ticked all three boxes. In my rundown leaking suite at the old colonial Strand Hotel in Rangoon, I found it driest to stand in the tub during the monsoon showers and, to get a beer, join one of the numerous wedding parties held at the hotel on a daily basis. Comfortable in comparison to the hut in the state of Gujarat with my new friend Guja, a rat! That stay in '88 I thought over again while helping the

ONGC seismic crew perfect their three-dimensional acquisition techniques with their UNHCR bequeathed Geocor IV ™ system. The very same system that I had taken delivery of in the docks of Bombay in '85 and offloaded in the foothill town of Dehradun.

****

Being in a new city with Adrian was good fun, as the neutral surrounding brought open and lively conversation which, when not about his work, was consumed by the twentieth-century history that engulfed the city of Volgograd. We visited the solitary building that survived the onslaught of the German 4th Army and went on to see the commemorated rifle used by the honoured Russian sniper, Vasily Zaytsev, on display in the Red Army museum. The experience was so arresting with the weight of history that, over our numerous bar breaks, we managed to reduce the catastrophic site to our childhood images of the *Victor* comic strip, this being for us the only legible image to comprehend the total destruction and survivalist lifestyle for those held up and dug in along the right bank of the Volga River, entombed by bomb blasts and frozen by winter.

His two plus year stay to focus on Volgograd had been explained to me by Andy as a long promised and negotiated release of product cargos from ex-Lukoil personnel, with whom Adrian had built a working relationship. This product would be countertraded on behalf of the local government for hard currency that was required for the construction of a trans Volga River bridge. This all seemed credible and worth the lengthy wait. Crude or petroleum product that would and could be lifted by VSTT amongst others and transported through to the Black Sea, similar to that traded a few years earlier. However, on reaching his comfortable top floor apartment of modest Soviet proportions, I was rather taken aback by an introduction to a woman by the name of Vita. Vita had been mentioned by Adrian in past discussions for her excellent translating, interpretation and local contact knowledge but not for her family planning aptitude, or lack thereof, as without too much gynaecological thought, I could make her out to be in her eighth month of pregnancy. I could sense and enjoy their happiness with all the expectation and planning that comes with this family state. I did not feel obliged or in a position to question the wisdom or conflict that this union created with his family in Ireland or his colleagues in Geneva, as both parties were waiting patiently for news of a product delivery. But not, I feared, this product!

Back at headquarters in Sardinia Street, London, we worked on the shipping cash flow and our ability to continue voyage charters over the months and into the spring with Glencore product, so long as they continued to discharge in the Caspian port of Neka, Iran. The program was confirmed and would benefit both John and Sharif who had developed the relationship with Navion, the Norwegian shipping group who were interested in developing the next class of Caspian tankers. The new tanker class would be of a size and capacity that was unable to enter or exit the Caspian the consequence of which was that each tanker required construction, dry docking and breaking all within the confines of the Caspian Sea. Together we could create a joint enterprise of their nautical architectural and capital strength, alongside our local shipping experience and contact base, especially with the National Shipping Company of Iran that could advance Navion's impressive foresight and conceptual business vision into reality.

Meanwhile, in the event that we could draft an acceptable agreement that would meet with both our returns and Russian legal standard, Brian and I concentrated on the expansive opportunities that the relationship with Andrey and Sunfloat Trading would offer. I also spent time with the Heritage Group, who were close to making their first trip to the Congo Brazzaville which would require representation from Tacoma and, therefore, a request for me to be present. For my own account, Alistair had made me constantly aware of their desire – and the collective need for – a full legal restructuring of VSTT up to and including the imposition of a new name, for the sake of the representation and reputation of the group. The Private Equity individuals among us, with genuine capital project experience, knew that the JOA 'loan' agreement from Mobil had a shelf life very much dependent on the performance of the project. This project was building a large and complex cost base that would, in a relatively short time, release a tectonic shift sufficient to question the existence and stability of VSTT or the newly named company (Newco). We estimated that the Mobil loan would retire over the next year, or within eighteen months at best, based on our judgement of the performance of the PSA. The timing and prospect was well discussed and documented at our meetings along with action to prepare for this event. This was both new territory for me and territory that I could not be seen by the Sumo boys to fail, as I knew their daggers were drawn and ready.

The Tacoma/Heritage visit to Brazzaville was well planned and attended over the daily meetings by the energy ministry officials who took to Tim's pleasant colonial style with polite, schoolboy attitude and interest. They seemed to enjoy the attention, in the presence of British aristocracy, which I thought odd given that their own past colonial masters were French and they were getting to experience the English colonial idiosyncrasies and dogmatic tones. Whatever their reasoning, they gave Tim their full attention and provided him with all the requisite data and support that would be expected under the circumstances. They accepted his political rhetoric and financial questions with expressions of downtrodden, submissive silence. Tim demonstrated his experience and did not lose his patience when dealing with African issues and culture. I knew however, that all would be revealed at the morning coffee when Andy would provide a summary of his meeting with the finance minister where the real issues would have been raised and resolved, in addition to all of Tim's pertinent questions. Andy likewise was happy with the trip result, as the additional trading volumes which had been confirmed would raise his corporate profile in line with his upstream approach. He also learnt from his source that his old firm and business adversary, Addax, were on his tail as they, on learning of Tacoma's new approach, were likewise looking to participate in upstream investment opportunities for a similar end gain. I considered this a good result, as time was of the essence and competition demanded decisions and favours be met. I was witnessing the revival of the early twentieth-century Standard Oil business-building technique returning to the African continent.

Over a short interlude in London, I met with Alistair and the legal firm Sinclair, Roche & Temperley, who had, up to that date, been the mouthpiece and legal correspondence for all Sumo related transactions, including the drafting and incorporation of VSTT. They had performed well I thought, based on my limited knowledge of shipping and corporate law. However, they had not been forthright in their opinions regarding Alistair's outline of a future newco: to incorporate not just a shipping interest but also focus on a structure which could (hopefully) hold high net worth core assets which had been developed through continued investment and growth by private equity investors. I hoped, finally, for a transparent corporate structure and profile that addressed the geographic diversity and fiscal liability reflective of the nature and operation of the company, inclusive but not limited by counter-majority voting clauses which would serve to ensure that the voice of the small, private shareholder was heard over the boom of the large, institutional shareholder. We left it with them to consider and draft a mandate letter for my return, as I was in progress to Saratov with Brian to engage with Andrey's chosen party and related business colleague, Alexey Bandorin.

The city of Saratov on the right and European bank of the Volga may be viewed as a poorer relation to its cousins, Samara and Volgograd, sitting to the northeast and south respectively. During the reign of Catherine the Great, the city and location was the transhipment hub for grain harvested from the emerging agricultural revolution developing over the eastern Steppes. The agricultural revolution was achieved through a government-controlled migration policy and settlement of German peasants in the 18th century. It continued its agrarian existence and growth throughout the social revolution of the 20th century, but did not attract or reach the industrial base that both Samara and Volgograd attained. The oblast or provincial authority and governor, according to Alexey, were corrupt at the local police but not corporate level and the corruption tended to focus on the movement of commodities. This piece of information, in hindsight, was not properly explored or exploited by me in the context of our project development or Alexey's health, both on the quasi-legal and practical basis. Brian and I were excited with our new playground that stretched 575 kilometres to the southeast and 330 kilometres from north to south.

This area, designated the 31st Russian state, was a proven hydrocarbon province since Soviet days with prospective Devonian and Carboniferous resource plays and concepts associated in and around the Pre-Cambrian basin. Academic concepts which, if proven correct, could lead to the identification and location of analogous anomalies to the great hydrocarbon fields discovered in Soviet times, such as the giant Tengiz Devonian reef oil and gas field operated by Chevron that lay on the southern rim of the same basin in neighbouring Kazakhstan.

Our introductory meetings, through interpreters, with the state owned Geological & Geophysical firm Nyshnivolkgeophysica were an uphill learning experience for both parties. At first, I was confused by the lack of understanding between us and assumed that it was due to poor translation. From my experience of similar Turkmen meetings, I had by then acquired a basic Russian fluency for the technical words used when describing geological features, wells, horizons, numerical depth and topography and could understand the translation, but their sense or meaning was not comprehensible to me, which was my problem. I thought it might simply be a personality issue or, more concerning, that a higher authority had already pronounced a verdict. If that were right, there was no overcoming the decision. Following numerous breaks and discussions back with Saphonos, the managing director, I still could not understand their intransigent technical position, which was a barrier to mutual respect and future co-operation.

Clarity and mutual understanding came following a side room conversation between Brian and their chief geologist that had focused on a highly technical and crucial element of prospecting in any region: the question and answer to the source of the hydrocarbon and its origin, or diagenesis (the organic physical and chemical changes occurring during the conversion of sediment to sedimentary rock). Under Soviet academic code, this erudite and important topic was determined on the centralised philosophical view and academic approach that varied from our western view, as theirs, state by state, or oblast by oblast, anointed a methodology which directed exploration staff to follow regardless of what the data may indicate. We concluded that their interpretative methodology and resulting prioritisation of a commercial prospect was derived from a top-down reasoning, whilst our western approach was bottom-up.

By the fourth morning, I noticed our consulting colleague appear at breakfast, shaking and damp. I assumed that, like us, he had bathed or taken a strip wash from the freezing water drawn directly from the frozen solid Volga River that caused ice cream headaches, especially when washing the hair. But no, this chap was suffering from a serious hangover. Sadly, we had brought the lad to his nirvana, being, as he was, an alcoholic who was suffering badly. His loss notwithstanding, Brian and I had concluded privately that Nyshnivolkgeophysica's professional and financial existence was in doubt due to lack of state funding. We therefore proposed an organisational chart that incorporated all the facets of a western exploration team which, funded by VSTT and subject to our veto on final well location, would duplicate their staff numbers, experience and capabilities. The outstanding problem that remained was to draft a binding document that would address our mutual interest and allow us all to move forward.

Chapter 12
Burren is Born

A wonderful extracurricular meeting and opportunity to acquaint myself with Roland Shaw came from the Tacoma/Heritage joint venture relationship. Roland was the ex-Chairman of Premier Oil, then a leading independent exploration and production company with interests in the North Sea, USA & Far East. A public figure renowned for his American straight-talking manner who was reaching the end of his chairmanship tenure and patience with Heritage majority shareholder and trouble shooter, Tony Buckingham. Roland was well liked by the city for his public statements and outbursts, but less so for his financial management skills. He was a kind and generous man, both with his time and purse, who enjoyed building business through personal relations amongst the younger community which provided opportunities for entrepreneurial thinkers and individuals. Similar to my appreciation of Atul Gupta as a future CEO when I met him at my first Monument Oil management meeting in 1994, moved on to the current resident manager for Monument in Turkmenistan, I saw Roland as the future chairman of Newco, a role that I would, in time, welcome him into.

We reached and passed the Effective Date for the Turkmen PSA on the 1st February 1997 without fanfare or celebration. It was probably right that the powers on the ground concentrated on meeting the obligations so that the authorities could be assured that the activity was projecting the ministry's expectations. At Sardinia House, we could have sat and waited for the first quarterly financial review with trepidation and noted that the crude price had dropped to a monthly average of $20.85 per barrel, but we had better things to get under way. We took to Moscow for legal exploratory meetings in an attempt to reach a draft co-operation agreement that would satisfy a pathway forward for both Kotor Tepe and Saratov.

At Norton Rose, a Moscow based international legal firm, we presented our thoughts and ideas for a working arrangement that would address the limitations of Russian petroleum law inclusive of a loan facility-financing instrument to obfuscate VAT as the central theme. The loan could be collateralised against crude oil reaching the wellhead or the collection tank. Under western standard accounting and audit terminology, the net asset value of the commodity may be attributed as core value on the balance sheet when the nominee of the balance sheet has legal title to that commodity. We knew that this was not a foreseeable legal event and therefore proposed that title ownership could be equated to operator control. Control of finance and logistics was supreme, we argued, and therefore warranted accreditation by the auditor through that control.

Our methodology to remunerate the host party alongside the contractor party was similar in design to a PSA agreement. That is, the Host received a percentage value from the monthly or quarterly revenue as royalty before a greater percentage pool of the revenue was used to repay the historic Contractor cost. The remainder or profit pool of the revenue would be split along agreed percentage terms. The profit percentage paid the Contractor loan which, under Russian tax law, would avoid VAT and could be repatriated. The beauty in this proposal, amongst others, was that the majority of the operational, geological and administrative (G&A) costs would be paid to the Host as they would be complying with and providing most all the subcontracting services, except for tools and technical requirements ordered from western suppliers. There would be one abiding requirement to our Joint Co-Operation Agreement (JCA) proposal: trust.

Brian and I travelled on to Saratov to continue the technical process, which we both felt had merit once it was given legal and accounting clearance for our proposed JCA. Our rounds of technical meetings generated positive momentum and clear acknowledgement that our draft JCA firmly demonstrated our commitment to provide funding and technical assistance to their G&A departments and service organisation upon our agreement to a drill location. We were convinced that the merger of the JCA agreement document and the local people of Saratov, as in Turkmenistan, were capable of achieving our joint objective.

Our band should have been called 'Bleak House' to reflect those bluesy recession days of 1994 when four unemployed professionals gathered to jam tribute blasts of favourite oldies. The distraction led amazingly to paid gig performances where the payment covered rental of PA equipment and travel costs for the lead guitarist Quentin, who was really on his downers. In April '97, the band had its highest gross fee performance at a 25th wedding anniversary around the Surrey hills of Godalming. Arriving suited, as it was a black-tie event in an erected tent, and shown into the library to wait our moment gave me time enough to learn that the event was primarily hosting London's independent oil and gas community. Later, on stage and thumping out the bass line to the good and great modern classics, I noted the long enquiring and confused stares from dancing members of the Monument Oil team, my partners in Turkmenistan. Without returning a hint of recognition, I managed to pass off the evening in total anonymity. Over the following days and weeks at partner meetings, the possibility that I had or needed a bass playing sideline was never mentioned nor was the possibility of my doppelgänger being seen about town.

In Ashgabat later that month, Sharif and I were guests amongst the family and friends of Mr Kulniazov, with whom we had expected to make the trip up to Nebit Dag for formal discussions. Sharif had learnt that he had returned to celebrate his fiftieth at home with his family in the capital and managed to get us an invitation. Just as important, Sharif had also managed to find a suitable birthday present – a super jumbo bottle of Johnnie Walker scotch. Laden with this enormous bottle we entered his walled Kremlin abode where the festivities were well underway. The huge man, an Olympian wrestler and State hero, was himself seated amongst his male family members surrounded by underlings and staff. Our welcome was exactly as expected for a foreign party to a Central Asian festivity where the women serve in silence and men toast in continuous and monotonous tones, customised to their relationship as family or friend or work and spoken from a lying or standing position depending on the intensity and dedication of the toast. Most all were made standing given the status and authority of our host. The initial and traditional five toasts to president, host, woman, nation and guests were then followed by long and ever depreciating content value before entering a European phase of disrespectful shouting. I was proximal to my host, Kulniazov, which permitted casual commentary and the occasional business thrust to discussing our desire to enter into formal negotiations with our JCA draft proposal which would enable us to participate in the future development of the Kotor Tepe Field. Happily, my efforts were sufficient and unobtrusive in context with the occasion.

All normality and formality were lost as dancing commenced and gathered pace of a quality that was inversely proportional to the stately occasion. My host's middle-aged wife took a shine to me and my dancing, which induced my princely Turkmen host to engage his suitor in a 'friendly' wrestling wager. Not since Custer circled his men has a more stupid act of defiant encouragement and bravado occurred. Despite clear auditory lines from Sharif as to my host's Olympian past, I still insisted on a wager: The winner taking the Kotor Tepe field. In jest or not, the proposal was irrational and provocative.

I woke in a shack close by, with the party still ringing in my ears and a thirst that was only suppressed by nervous commands to both my upper limbs to move, but neither limb would budge. Not for the last time Sharif, similar to three years earlier, had to greatly assist me over the next two days in the basics as both my lower forearms lay prone at my side. He told me many times how I had lost the field and the use of my arms. The latter was only temporary but the former was permanent, as negotiations, Turkmen style, were complete.

Sharif stayed in Ashgabat to procure effects and make housekeeping chores around town for Sapar and the company, while I headed off with Sapar the driver, to recuperate in the field and make an unsupervised visit to the Burun field and facility. Meeting with Guildev in Nebit Dag town, I learnt how our recent developments in the area, which had brought with them the constant arrival of expatriate and contractor personnel, had been coolly received by the local community: undoubtedly, it had benefited the area with the purchase or rental of accommodation but, as yet, it had not brought regular employment. I made the point that the initial phase of the work program would be dedicated to a 3-dimensional seismic survey which should provide medium term employment. Guildev, my new friend and old acquaintance from the first tour in 1993, had remained in Nebit Dag with the chief field engineer and his hospitable family residing off the main square in town. He was always the perfect host and confidante in all matters, which allowed me to contribute to local matters and maintain good relations with the authorities.

Through confusion or desire, I missed my return flight and rebooked for another from Ashgabat three days later. Without Sharif and with no agenda I took up Murad's kind offer of his apartment. We enjoyed each other's company and I spent much time contemplating the name of the Newco, which would be required on my return for inclusion in the draft restructuring documents. My obvious Irish name indicated an Irish provenance and I felt that association should be acknowledged. We already had Aiden Heavey and Tullow, the recent loss of an Arran and, given my Galway University association, the naturalness of both the botanical flora and geological strata found on the southern coastline of Galway Bay in the neighbouring Burren came to my mind. The unique nature of the region and name brought the passing thought to prominence. In my self-imposed isolation, I played with the name 'Burren Energy' and its possible transformations or abbreviations, which led so enjoyably to projecting the dominant flower found over the karstic landscape – a simple Orchid – as my company emblem and Mr Roland Shaw CBE as my Chairman.

The Burren orchid logo

Chapter 13
Simply the Best

The corporate restructure flow chart produced by Sinclair Roche & Temperley (SRT) simply did not stand up to the scrutiny of either Alastair or my personal legal advisor, Jonathan Pym, a partner with Travers Smith Braithwaite (TSB) who, also being Diana's brother-in-law and knowing of my strained financial circumstances, was kindly acting for Balor Holdings pro bono. It was hard to understand why they were not up to the job but, just possibly, SRT were being impeded by directives from Michael and Simon, who were proving costly to the drafting process. With the need for expediency, the mandate was taken from SRT and, with a VSTT board majority vote in favour, given to TSB. This course of action left me bereft of my advisor, who was released accordingly to handle our corporate mandate.

We moved forward swiftly, identifying the offshore domicile domain to satisfy the respective liability for our portfolio of companies, all of which could collectively and legally operate under a UK holding company – Burren Energy Plc. Jonathan kindly had my Balor Holdings Ltd mandate transferred to Farrer & Co, also of Lincoln's Inn Field and who, on the initial interview, came straight to the point and asked 'how did I, a man introduced to them as a bit of an "Indiana Jones", get to know Jonathan Pym'? I replied cheerily that 'we knew the same girls.'

We co-opted Roland onto the board of the new company as Chairman over a good lunch at Sarastro's which pleased Michael no end, as Roland's rather immense physique and appetite made Michael's positively modest in comparison. It was apparent to me then, that despite the side-line barracking and cries of foul play, Michael alone was a positive contributor to our mutual business development, but when with and under the spell of Simon, he became a very effective sea anchor. Their obstructive games, which took the form of legal letters demanding responses, made matters even more difficult and costly as the company's immediate purpose was to raise new capital. This capital was required to fund our 25% working interest in the Burun PSA and we estimated that we needed it by mid-1998 or possibly sooner, should the crude price continue to fall inversely to operation expenditure. Baring Investment Bank, who had the capital-raising mandate, wanted to raise the necessary funds to meet our cash requirements for the emergent Burren Energy through their private equity clients.

The ordeal of city meetings – the white collar, tie and Mr Suites (his real name) – was a completely disorientating experience, as was moving through the rarefied offices of the city where interest dwindled to non-existent upon detail of the geography. Our next and more successful move was over to Boston and New York, where my name and provenance proved more of a draw card than the story. Sufficient funds were raised from new private equity entrees, Capital International, Pictet and Baupost, to satisfy our estimated equity holding and growth for the foreseeable future. Together with BVCP, Burren Energy had, in its short existence, collected a premium group of international institutional shareholders and board members alongside a proven collection of sweat equity equivalent. Despite the infighting, and the addition some twelve months later of one further world class institution (AIG), this completed the institutional board members and tight shareholding up to moments before a public listing on the London Exchange.

I was never at all clear whether Michael and Simon's difficult attitude was simply due to their dislike of me or fear of throwing away their equity as a consequence of their past management decisions. I understood from Sumo chatter that most of their holding in the original company, Sumo Transportation & Trading, and its successor, VSTT, had been exchanged for debt on poor exchange terms to the Tsakos family, as the share register at the point of restructuring showed Tsakos, through Chios Energy, in ascendency, which materially diluted Michael and Simon's interest.

Roland took up his new office and domestic duties like a newly returned colonial uncle in constant need of a good lunch. He introduced me to his city acquaintances with no other purpose than to provide a fertile platform to tell my story. A story which resonated with some as a company that had an interesting past and firm future, and to others as a company with a narrow commercial beam which lacked diversity and could be easily broadsided by the political geography of the region. I expected these views to be tested at my first public corporate presentation, arranged by Roland with the Independent Oil and Gas Group at their monthly meeting, which was held on a weekday evening in the city. My presentation was a resounding failure. I confused my pitch with detail when just a high-level view of the streamlined body of the endeavour would have been sufficient. Fortunately, only the few, including Sharif and Roland, made the show and no questions or comments were taken from the gallery as there was no gallery present. I was extremely grateful to Roland for taking me through that gate and into the public arena. I had past experience in public speaking during events at Geophysical conventions in Los Angeles and Melbourne, yet quietly feared the moment and the occasion. Like many before and since, as the progenitor of a company I was ill prepared for criticism and judgement or blame, which is the privilege of the city and investment community to confer.

A clear road to financial growth and corporate diversity was my desired mantra. With increasing expenditure in Turkmenistan, the opportunity for expansion in shipping, transportation and trading throughout the Caspian and Russian River system could found relationships upon which to build upstream opportunities in Russia. This proven plan had the capacity to broaden Burren beyond the Caspian, but it lacked diversification away from the endemic regional political risk. The diversity that I was looking for, by chance, became reality in the Congo Brazzaville as Tacoma and Heritage moved the PSA discussions up to the final level.

The inclusion of a large exploration permit area, which extended northwest from the Kouakuala producing area, along the coastal escarpment onshore section to the Louess River was a critical and positive step forward. Upon reaching a draft agreement with the Ministry, as is so often the case in business, the competition arrived in the name of Ranger Oil: a Canadian company based in Calgary with interests in Angola that I suspected were present because of Heritage, who also had, through Tony Buckingham, interests in Angola. Andy and I travelled along with Tim from Heritage for a (Energy) ministerial 'standoff', the sole purpose of which was to improve the minister's bonus. Throughout the day, both teams, along with their local representative, made presentations to the energy minister and his officials, pleading that their 'money' was better. Phil Dimmock, leading the Ranger team, made their pitch, which was wonderfully undermined by the circulating story of his Canadian Chairman opening a gala dinner in Calgary for their Angolan representatives with 'I would like to welcome our Mongol friends to…' Yet it was Andy's night-time chat to the finance minister, as seemed custom, that sealed the deal and allowed the announcement that Tacoma/ Heritage had signed the PSA the following morning. Whatever the purpose or rationale that Buckingham was playing, it soon manifested itself into a corporate duel that only had one winner: Tim, the man who had brought Heritage the business, was left without a position in the company as Buckingham had made himself Chairman of Heritage Oil and Gas with Mike Wood as CEO.

Through 1998 and into 1999, the value of most all commodities, including oil, fell on the commodity markets over the world through an unspecified cause. However, this event would change the industry skyline and, for us lesser mortals, our byways and alleyways in the extreme.

Without budgetary concern, the operation in Turkmenistan moved past the seismic acquisition and preliminary real estate, road and field construction phases into a full-blooded intensive capital and operation expenditure program befitting of a major western oil company. Despite our out-voted cries at the joint management meetings for more local participation and fewer expatriates, the levels of western contractor noise increased to include two drilling 'work-over' rigs on daily rates, all tubular consumables, vehicles from western suppliers as well as western construction of all road and site facility and accommodation units. There was a general green light for all expenditure that got the desired effect in the corridors of the Energy Ministry, where their national strategy saw benefit and reason to cheer as our incremental oil production ramped over a contractual line that, in January '98, proved to be our first foreign contractor oil under the terms of the PSA. Good as it was to achieve foreign contractor oil under the terms of the PSA, the costs were prohibitive and unsustainable given the net back sale price. In contrast to our operation in Saratov, Brian and I had veto on the technical decisions, which left all aspects of the operation, logistics and choice of equipment to our local partner. Without doubt, our approach was slower, seasonal and modest, but, knowing our legally non-binding agreement, it gave us the opportunity to monitor their performance on a monthly basis and address the weakening commodity price.

Movement into and around the Caspian had increased air travel to the region, as numerous European airlines tested one or other route to support the emerging activity in the market. I caught a Lufthansa flight from Ashgabat via Baku with my usual 'seaman' ticket: a discounted ticket for the terminal rear end seat of a plane reserved for returning maritime crew. I was enjoying the tranquillity of the empty galley – that is, right up until my solitude was interrupted by a jacket whose pattern is only on offer to cause seizure or to suit the tastes of new-money

Russians. Helmut Mayrhofer introduced himself, said that he knew who I was and that my work was well known to his company of traders from our activity within the transportation sector. He then proceeded to lecture me on the faults and limitations of my approach. In his view, there was so much more that could be achieved with the capital assets and connections I had. I didn't disagree and responded, as only one can to such Germanic confidence, with an offer to join the company. He 'would be delighted' was his reply and we had a drink to welcome him aboard.

Helmut's appearance and willingness to join us was nothing more than prophetic, as within weeks of his arrival Mike Calvey, after a quick beer together, would table a business proposition to the Burren board to offer Burren Energy Shipping and Transportation (BEST) a 15-year bare boat charter on 16 Volgoneft vessels. Mike proposed that his Baring Vostok Capital Partners (BVCP) would transact the charter, being the majority board of Volgotanker, and 'sell' to BEST for new stock in the Burren Energy Plc. Company. This opportunity, for John and Sharif to manage a fleet of 16 vessels in conjunction with an in-house trader was not just a 180 degree turn back to the original business plan, but a far more aggressive equivalent: giving them control of crew and vessel at a time when the commodity prices for product within the region were declining to an historic low.

Generational events for our industry that year had begun with the BP purchase/merger of Amoco in August. Without industry support, the commodity price declined to levels that questioned the valuation of high cost producing assets, namely offshore North Sea, along with many new overrunning budget development projects similar to ours in Turkmenistan. The following December, with huge implications to Burren, Exxon acquired Mobil; the average crude price for the year fell to $11.91 per barrel. Further concern for the resource sectors was, as a quote attributed to a Shell Oil executive in Time Magazine that autumn stated, "Shell expected the price to fall to $3.00 per barrel". The Exxon merger had the desired effect of stalling expenditure on the PSA project while a change of the partner management team took place, but this was sadly insufficient to stem the cash haemorrhage.

I was in no position to control the outflow of cash as demands from the Turkmen PSA Joint Operating Committee had to be met, which resulted in my hand being forced to request – and thankfully receive – a penally high interest working capital loan from our faithful shareholder, Mike Calvey at BVCP. His attitude was fair in so far as BVCP were our largest shareholder and yet, in his view, not the banker of choice for its other institutional equity holders. Mike had taken the mantle of instructional control over the board. Richard Sobel certainly saw and took this opportunity to invest in Sumo and my Game Plan business model. Yet it took Mike Calvey and his vehicle, BVCP, time to build its position, through stealth and design, into the dominant player and wealth generator that it would become for both Burren and BVCP shareholders alike. Mike was a unique American overseas: a young man, 32, from Tulsa, Oklahoma that could only continue to impress in both formal and fun company. With his pleasant intellect, personal and gracious business style, he was an antidote to the arrogance and intimidation filling other chairs around our board table. His common-sense investment approach won him the admiration and confidence of his private equity industry colleagues and peers at Burren and indeed, amongst the majority of his Russian colleagues under his BVCP umbrella based in Moscow. He would, over time, build the largest private equity investment house of funds dedicated to the former Soviet Union region. His confident style, I believe, could also be his Achilles heel as, with or without intention, Mike's relaxed charm often concealed the ambitious businessman within, often taking his business partners and associates by unhappy surprise.

And so, over those dark winter months and into the new year, whilst holding our position at the PSA table and, as predicated, with a fifteen-year bare boat charter for 16 river-sea Volgoneft tankers signed, we put together a program that would change the trading geography of the Eastern Caspian and southern Russian river system. This program would commence coincident with the opening of the canal, as sixteen vessels under John's management steamed to load ports nominated under Helmut's master plan to purchase cargo using the funds that BVCP thought were going to the upstream PSA, but were in fact destined to a 'mothership' located at a point yet to be finalised by Sharif in the Azov Sea.

The operation on my crook shoulder had gone well according to the surgeon, as the tangled and twisted nerve mess from a dislocation while body surfing off Perth in 1991 had been corrected and would heal well in time. While still under postoperative care and in serious pain, I discharged myself from Princess Anne's Southampton University Hospital and proceeded straight to meet John Stanton at Heathrow for the flight to make an appointment with the Tsakos shipping team in Greece. Good old Captain Panagiotis Taskos was as good as I had always heard and took John and myself though to his inner sanctum, where I could rest as he could see that I was in pain. The importance of our trip was as clear as my drugged-up mind could muster: to charter a mothership suitable to our needs and Sharif's plan. John, who had spent time with the Taskos fleet, knew of an elderly lady – a tanker which was destined for scrap. Our needs and their interest in the company took prime charge as Captain P. altered the vessel's final plans to allow us to charter the 95,000-ton tanker at a beneficial rate for the navigational period (March through to November) of the Russian river system on the agreement that, thereafter we would pay to deliver the vessel to their desired scrap location.

In February 1999, the Tsakos tanker, Maria, dropped sea anchors within the international bonded waters in the Kerch Strait off Crimea to await the arrival of the first transhipment cargoes from the BEST Volgoneft fleet. Each cargo secured amongst her 35 segregated storage tanks according to product type and forward sale.

The Transhipment operation in progress

Chapter 14
Better than all the Rest

The poor months for the industry continued through 1999, as company after company retrenched and reviewed their asset portfolio and capital expenditure. Following on my experiences in 1982 and 1986, this was my third and most severe confrontation with a period of a low commodity price environment and, similar to the last time in Australia, it required innovative action.

By almost any international experience and operation standard, the transhipment and trading operation that BEST commenced that spring was more than innovative: it was majestic, theatrical and cash generative. The product market in the region was plumbing the depths when a ton of low sulphur fuel oil could be bought on the Ashgabat commodity exchange for $17 ton (Free on board – FOB). Exclusivity to purchase was given to those few operators with proven vessel capacity. The products could be shipped through to the Black Sea ports and sold for $75 ton (Cost inclusive of freight – CIF). The BEST business concept operated in conjunction with Helmut's choice of transhipped products including, but not limited to, high and low sulphur fuel oils, VGO, diesel oil, Jet A-1 aviation fuel, high and low sulphur crude oils and cooking oils. In each outgoing trade from the Mothership – *Maria* – Radi & Godfried, a team of product traders based in Zug, Switzerland, would arrange the sale of a specific cocktail product that was mixed over the transhipment process to a third and larger vessel (=+ 50,000ton) that would berth alongside the *Maria*. The off-taking vessel would then sail to a discharge destination within the Mediterranean or, as in a few cases, as far as New York or Singapore where the price would reach in excess of $200 ton CIF, in the case of low sulphur products.

This concept and operation was so prosperous that its success would in time cause retribution and objection from the large and truculent Russian producers and exporters from whom we were purchasing the majority of our product. They would conspire to take over and replace our system with their own, which, by 2002, they did. From a corporate perspective, the operation was not core to the business value, but the loss of the scheme was sad from a personal perspective with the twin loss of three extremely good cash generative river navigation seasons and boyhood dreams.

However, over that period, the BEST team grew with the volumes transhipped. Jennifer Simonson (nee Argemen), a confident self-driven lady from the Sumo melee joined John and Sharif, which elevated immediately their profile within the region, especially with the training required for the early Kazakhs crews and her direct East-End London no-prisoner-taken style. Helmut took advantage of his single status to introduce numerous Turkmen, Ukraine and Croatian ladies into his trading team, all of whom prospered both within the team and even more so in their later careers. Jennifer went on to join the Chevron International marine group in Houston which, in my view, must have been a pinnacle moment to that date for a self-financed night school scholar.

In the upstream world of business, the mood was a wet Monday in February only made interesting by the announcement that our operator and partner in the Burun PSA had been bought by another London based oil and gas company – Lasmo. Within a matter of four months, we at Burren had lost both of our Turkmen partners through hostile or agreed takeovers. This changed not only the personnel but also the corporate chemistry of the partnership. Gone was the friendly attitude of Mobil to be replaced with the monolithic straight jacketed, sterile face of Exxon. To add to this was the loss of the acceptably arrogant and chippy attitude of Monument, as we were faced yet again with a management that didn't even wish to meet with us thinking we were only an irritation, which was a huge sadness.

I did see one ray of sunshine, that I followed straight to Ashgabat to bathe in its warmth: I went to speak with Atul. In his position as General and Country Manager for Monument, he had led the corporate strategy partner relationship with Mobil in their joint Turkmen business developments. As such, he had not been seen as approachable or considered a visible partner to Burren. He had shown his good will to us through his silence, having not made any attempt to denigrate our position in the eyes of the Turkmen authorities, as other members of his executive had. I had enjoyed the opportunity with Sharif, late the previous autumn, to make a curry with Atul at his Ashgabat home and watch a World Cup football match, which allowed us the time to better understand each other. With his position under review following the Lasmo takeover and his opportunities muddied with the loss of his peer and friend Tony Craven Walker, I thought he may well give his situation some thought and find cause to jump.

I had stuck to my Mao 'little red book' view and, over the relatively short period of the PSA term, I had not approached Atul with any social overtones other than the curry night. I did sense that since our initial meeting five years earlier, my entrepreneurial energies and the spectacle of Burren had been spent. However, gladly, the company's future style would be viewed as being at an acceptable level of professional development: job security, financial security and the potential equity returns from a start-up going into the public market. Atul could evaluate Burren and its evolving financial security given his inside knowledge of the Burun PSA and its potential. It would be Atul's insight into Burren's current and potential future which pushed him to make the move to join us. I obviously withheld details of the shareholder and fiscal difficulties, but I knew that he had insight into the history and current relations with Michael and Simon, as would have been gleaned from gossip with his 'good lunch' going colleagues over the years. He indeed was up to date with the recent new institutional shareholder additions and the board strength of BVCP, all of whom had taken the time to perform due diligence on Burren, including a meeting with Atul on their country visit or when in London. We concluded that Atul would be pleased to join us with the official position of Chief Operating Officer (COO), starting at a time beneficial to him. This suited my options as I would have to lay a new setting at the board table, make room in our cosy office space and, awaiting his arrival and appointment, I had the perfect man on the inside over the interim period as both new partners, Exxon and Lasmo, took control of the situation.

The technical teamwork in Saratov had identified a well location which, if successful, would prove a commercial play and sustain an ongoing drilling program. Brian and the team set to firm the location and prepared to mobilise a local rig. Communication between us and the Saratov concern was improved and maintained by a frequent visit from Adrian and his multitasking lady, Anya, both of whom were based in Volgograd. Adrian and Anya had become the logistical support for the established BEST regional office. Adrian had over the previous 12 months made the transition from Tacoma to BEST by mutual agreement between the parties. Given their enhanced status in the West African region, Tacoma redirected their destiny and future back to their existing base in trade and the potential upstream business.

Adrian's Tacoma time in the European-Russian sector would benefit the new business model for BEST, which required a full-on logistics team to support the fleet with canal and lock gate movements plus bunkering requirements. It also gave Adrian the opportunity, as he saw it, to pursue upstream ventures through his community contacts in the Volgograd and neighbouring Rostov region which, if agreeable to the parties, Burren would support on a partnership basis. Regrettably in my view, Adrian refused to join Burren as the regional manager in favour of his independent consultant status, even though it was made clear the former position would benefit him from the emerging corporate share option and bonus scheme. He decided to remain an independent and did so until his departure from Burren in the autumn of 2001 with the demise of the river fleet operations.

With spring and a hike in the oil price, life seemed to return to my shareholders and their egos. With no appreciation of the success of BEST or the loan package provided by, and soon to be repaid back to BVCP or the recent corporate events affecting our relations in Turkmenistan, a group of Burren shareholders wanted to replace Roland as Chairman with a more 'agile' fellow – Brian Lavers. Their demand was not contested given that Andrey and I, who enjoyed Roland and his tenure, were in no position to fight given Mike and Alistair both stood neutral on the motion. An ex-Chairman of Shell Nigeria was co-opted while, as a consolation to me, Roland remained on the board. The benefits were marginal, if any, but the noise for the gallery was tumultuous.

I do not know from whom the proposal originated, but given the timing, style and content, it most likely should be attributed to Atul given his inside knowledge of the PSA & JOA terms and the position of chief operating officer in waiting: Burren took the opportunity that was offered in the draft of the Joint Operating Agreement (JOA) which stated, 'following a three-year period and "Without Cause", the Operator of the Burun PSA could be reassigned to another partner to the JOA'. With the intention of becoming the nominated operator, Burren wrote a letter addressed to the head office of Exxon USA, then in Delaware, to request that it be nominated as the operator.

There followed a deathly period of silence only broken by a letter from Exxon requesting that we establish our credentials and identity as we were not a public company and therefore beyond their intelligence. As a small private company with limited corporate guarantee, this in itself created public liability issues for Exxon's international status. They would send a top-level team of executives to the UK to interview us. Panic ensued. I cannot confirm whether this action was the direct cause or effect of the action that Exxon took later that summer, in announcing that they were to resign or quit both the Production

Sharing Agreement (PSA) and Turkmenistan. The immediate effect of Exxon's relinquishment of their equity in the PSA and other documents, as well as the pre-emption rights under the law governing the Joint Operating Agreement, was an increase to our participating interest, as a proportion of their interest, by an additional 16.4% to bring our interest up to 41.4%.

As a result of Burren's increased participating interest, the London upstream investor and peer community base thought the PSA was failing and the Exxon action confirmed their earlier understanding of the PSA limitations from Monument's tenure as Operator. Burren firmly believed that a change to the operating manner and budget would revive the PSA performance and fortunes, but I was in no position to debate our view to the contrary, as my time was immediately dedicated to raising funds to meet the financial demands on Burren for our improved proportional interest.

Possibly as a hang-over from our initial capital raise, or perhaps as a consequence of my constant round of door knocking and pavement crawling since that time with Roland and our investment banker, in late September '99, we were quickly able to finalise a $6 million subscription from the international insurance group AIG, again US based, through their dedicated Central Asian Silk Road Fund. I took that moment to repay Mike's debt, through an equity conversion of the $4.0 million outstanding to the BVCP group's Cavendish Fund. Both transactions were priced at a $0.60 per share. While these events were ongoing, Atul left Monument Oil/Lasmo to join Burren.

By mid-navigation season in July '99, BEST had transported in excess of 120,000 tons of product and the talk from Volgotanker was of increasing the size of the fleet by up to 40 vessels for next year's season. I was not sure, as the dry dock cost per vessel was yet to hit our cash reserves given the seasonal nature and structure of the business. Money and time was required over the next three seasonal periods to dry dock and refurbish all 16 of the majority 8–22-year-old vessels.

This dry dock work was customarily done over the winter season in Astrakhan but could be undertaken in the Black Sea ports, should the vessel operate in winter months outside the Russian river system. I would have to consider this option clearly and carefully as the commitment was significant. I was by then more focused on the upstream business plan, which itself had grown exponentially in both Turkmenistan and more recently in Saratov, with the first well drilling having commenced but not expected to complete until the following spring. The transhipment operation was quite a brilliant piece of business for its time, yet it was not the core asset value that I knew barrels of crude in the ground could command. I was all too aware that my shareholders and recent additions were not with me to hear about ships and trading: share value was their interest and would only become more so as time progressed.

Chapter 15
Tour of Duty

Tectonic snoring along with the arctic cold made my circumstances, by any standard, a nightmare situation. The top bunk bed in a simple wooden cabin located over 1000kms north of Ulan Bator, had an open fire which, when alight, would yield 60°C above. But the room temperature would drop to 50°C below over the hour, as the fire burnt out and Andrey's snoring abounded. By the third night and with the onset of sleep deprivation, I took myself out into the backyard to lie in a coffin shaped box, quite possibly the real thing, just to escape the snoring. I rose from a delirious sleep before sunrise.

Already dressed in a Soviet winter infantry camouflage suit and my Chevron arctic coat with the wolverine coated 'south park' hood, and having sucked on some frozen salmon bits as my breakfast and drank a hot drink from 'frozen' fruit, I set out stalking along the deer tracks. Like the previous two mornings, the tracks led us straight to the lake's frozen banks where two splayed deer carcasses lay, eviscerated by wolves. Unlike the other mornings and simply due to exhaustion, I took a break on the high eastern viewing ledge surrounded by pinewoods that stand frozen and silent. I witnessed a pinch of light on the horizon, the focus of a soundless sunrise similar in the Sandy or Painted Desert or off the escarpment of Northern Somalia; but here, in and around the frozen state of Lake Baikal, the rays reaching those trunks would make the trees moan and sigh in a choral resonance echoing Einstein's principle of the photoelectric effect.

Later that morning, I met a jolly swagman: a local who pitched a fire and 'billy' tin can to make us tea as we learnt about the wild man's Scottish grandmother. I had recently read a book which had published extracts taken from five diaries of British women that had travelled in the pre-revolutionary period each with a position of nanny: a view of his grandmother's wandering with a purpose.

Our only real and beneficial sport was ice fishing on the lake, which provided me with the only non-frozen food of the trip, as the Baikal Lake endemic native fish – Omlu – was small and tasty when eaten raw directly from the water. With the extreme conditions prevailing, we made the three-hour return drive to Irkutsk, only to find I had Andrey as my roommate again. I spent that night rolled up within the carpet runner along the wide wooden breezy Siberian corridor and managed a good rest despite the rolling thunderous bouts emanating from my partner's room. Andrey and I decided, in favour of keeping our livers as another three days of drinking was not appealing, not to use our return tickets to Omsk on the Trans-Siberian railway and instead bought flights to Moscow. Enjoying coffee and brandy (then our custom for mornings with Murad in Ashgabat), we dwelt on a simple point of commerce that had huge implications to his financial future and investment style. How, he asked, do we realise money from our work and deeds in the Former Soviet Union (FSU)? By no means an expert myself, and only a few pages ahead in the book, I attempted to answer his question through the image of a virtual pipe stretching from the FSU to the city of London. In this imaginary pipeline, our subterranean crude reserves are grouped and summarised as proven producing barrels plus proven probable barrels – those barrels of crude that were confirmed through geological contact but are yet to be produced. Both groups were tabulated as our reserves. That collective reserve figure was fed through the FSU end whilst inflow through the virtual pipe was appraised and given a dynamic net asset value (NAV) to market for those barrels. A value that could simply be expressed as the net value per barrel less the cost of capital and operating per barrel discounted by the political risk. The NAV figure was then presented as a value in a share certificate which was given to you and me. Those shares could be held as collateral or not, or sold on the exchange in the city of London.

Andrey and I had both heard of an Oligarch*, as the term was then being bandied about but not really understood, which led to his next and more philosophical question: 'How does a capitalist continue to make money?' This was way above my pay grade, yet I answered simply that 'they live off the interest on the interest'. I knew that Andrey's espionage training had persuaded him of the view that the desired answer will only result from the correct question; happily, he seemed to be content with my responses. We both slept for the remainder of the six-hour flight.

News of the 100 ton (approximately 740 bopd) light daily crude flow rate from the Saratov well was a wonderful result considering the payback time of less than six months for a total well cost under $1.5 million, which was competitive when compared to our Burun PSA operated work-over well costs of over $5.0 million per well. We all feared for the day when a Burun new exploration well, budget and expenditure would be proposed, as we would no doubt need another shareholders whip-round. With the Saratov geological play concept and objective proved, Brian got board approval for the next two wells proposed, although questions were raised on the movement and marketing of the crude within the local market. We had no special export plan for the crude, other than keeping to our local working philosophy which expected our host partner to truck the crude produced to a local sale point where the revenue received in local currency would be set against the Joint Co-operation Agreement (JCA) account to cover local past and future expenditure, reduce the growth in our intercompany debt and, over time, be expatriated as roubles, which of course were fully convertible.

The Saratov success, BEST's 2000 transhipment program which included the charter of a 120,000-ton mothership tanker from Tsakos and the improved equity position in Turkmenistan were all extremely positive events. News from the African theatre that the civil disturbances in the 'broader' Congo were under control, was quickly followed with a request by the Republic of Congo Energy Ministry, or more likely through the new presidential office, that our partnership consider a proportional sale (farmout) of equity to a French colonial company – Maurel & Prom. This was an extremely beneficial opportunity for Tacoma, as the sale capital and terms received released Tacoma from their financial commitment to the new exploratory seismic survey, a well work-over and one new appraisal well in the Kouakouala production licence which they would otherwise have had to provide.

All this providence was indicative that the 21st century was looking bright and about to increase in luminosity over a lunch hosted by Richard Redmayne, not heard of since 1995 and who had moved on to HSBC bank. At lunch, Richard asked a throw away, possibly rhetorical question: would we be interested in buying the Lasmo interest in the Burun PSA? I blundered "yes", with a figure only to be corrected by Atul that we would, but for 'no charge' as we would also be accepting all their liabilities. This of course was a much better answer and made us all sit up and take note of the question.

Not long after that lunch, I was on the receiving end of a stern, unsolicited lecture with neither an offer of coffee nor refreshment, from the Lasmo project manager, Mark MacAlister. Sitting in his office, Mark addressed my 'tyrannical, exalted, contemptible Irish Catholic reputation amongst his circle of industry friends, which I took to mean that I was not perfect, and thereafter dismissed my company as undeserving. He eventually got to his point of business by stating that, as ill prepared as Burren may be under the circumstances, he had no other option given the 'failure of the project' than to negotiate Lasmo's departure from the PSA. He reiterated their willingness to negotiate with Burren rather than attempt a sale to a third party (in truth, probably due to pre-emption rights). What a wonderful moment as I kept my cool, confirmed that we would be back in touch soon and left delighted. My thoughts rushed to the potential that this opportunity to take commercial control without partners gave us: the full authority to reduce expatriate staff, cut all western contracts, quit the technical and expensive course of the incremental production program which had been in place over the past two year period, open the doors to both blue and white collar local workers and concentrate where we believed the immediate potential existed in exploring the shallow horizons using conservative local techniques while introducing extensive gas lift facilities to all existing producing wells. A dream as I left the Lasmo building which would become reality within a year.

The board meeting that soon followed to announce and act on the developments with Lasmo attempted to address all the fractions and factors which were influencing the moving parts on display. The meeting was chaotic and not helped by the absence of a finance director, I having just fired him. We had parted over a difference of opinion with regard to our cash position, future liquidity and the company's ability to continue to perform. The chap's ego had been massaged and entertained by the gallery over the past few months (if not the past year) and clearly felt under pressure from them to prevent further dilution of their holdings, which he perceived to be a terminal problem. I understood the problem but not his reaction, which was to direct the company toward administration. His action was entirely an overreaction brought about by his lack of trust in me, an in-depth knowledge of our field operations and, most important of all, a grasp of the support and willingness of our senior fully funded institutional shareholders. He failed to mention his concern or intentions to me, but rather managed to convince the new Chairman of our reduced corporate cash position, who in turn, told me.

The majority of the board voted to raise additional funds from a whip-round of existing shareholders, for an amount not less than $5 million and not more than $7million. This, I knew, was going to be difficult from my own Balor

Holdings perspective, as I was quite exhausted financially from the previous seven years and would not be able to subscribe personally. I therefore offered my Balor Holdings subscription rights to my 'friends & family' which was taken up in full. I was delighted to have family participation at last, especially my parents, and that it came at this stage in the project and corporate development as the risk then was only the commodity price, which was rising steadily.

Hywel John arrived looking the cardboard cut-out of a banker, a style in keeping to that of an intern with one of the big accounting firms but he was far from their dull image. Hywel made a perfect fit and addition to the growing spectrum of characters at Burren with his python-esque intellect and humour, Welsh tone and cartoon looks. As the new finance director, he immediately notched his mark with the introduction of a trade finance relationship with a new Swiss based bank in Lucerne to support BEST, which reduced our internal cash exposure and bounced our annual expectations for growth in trading products into reality. The finance program that he introduced went on to be the primary supporting finance package when, later that year, we commenced as operator and 100% equity owner of the exports from the Turkmen PSA, which required large capital inflow, most of which came from the juggling of the cash thrashing around the multiple trade finance deals.

I left the office hearing Helmut attempting to complete his new Russian visa application: 'Single – Yes, Married – Yes, Divorced – Yes' and set off for Samara that spring with John while Sharif headed for Kerch, in the Crimea. This left Atul, Hywel and Brian to carry through the PSA surrender terms with Lasmo. This was the right move, as Mr MacAlister's puritanical view was liable to become disturbed by my 'stealing' ways, so the further removed I was the better it could be concluded by the lads. The night at the burlesque show in Samara sealed the inclusion in the fleet of 16 Volgoneft vessels, the *Samara City* and *Astrakhan City* vessels for BEST, both being new builds from BVCP and Sumo finance. I remember the evening for the moment when, after a round of B-52 drinks had been taken, the festivities were interrupted as the muted cry 'fire!' was heard from behind. John's hand and glass along with the table's paper cloth were aflame as the burning B-52s spilt and spread onto the floor.

I saw the singular smoke stack on the horizon; in the Great Sandy Desert, this was indicative of an aboriginal signal of warning or attention, but here, on the eastern Steppes approaching the territorial boundary with Kazakhstan, it was a sign that could have only one meaningful answer given the approximate direction: a discovery well. For over an hour, we drove, my expectations growing with the smoke stack. We arrived on site to total chaos as the rig tried to launch itself upwards under the natural pressure of gas venting from below. The drama exploded as a roustabout member of the crew threw the fire rag over the gas pit which illuminated and cooked all within a 50-metre radius. In the confusion, I took note of the smoke's density and darkness to gauge liquid content, carbon calibration and value of the flow when stable, all of which were initially impressive from a commercial standpoint. I thought of value: value of the gold content amongst the cores in PNG, the crude filling the bunker in Okarem, the streak of crude down the white jacket on the Turkish flight and the value – the value of experiencing our second discovery.

I travelled on to Saratov to congratulate our local partners and discuss ongoing marketing issues, only to experience another first: a television interview alongside the local boss about the concern. An opportunity for much self-congratulation for him and a monotone diatribe from me about the valued joint-cooperation and the diligence of our relationship, all of which, I blundered on, being founded on trust. I possibly overstated the point to obsession. Taking my leave the following day, I headed for Volgograd to collect Adrian, Anya and Vita for an extremely pleasant drive along the Don River scenery, which was Gainsborough country with tree lined roads, fields and river all worked by village locals and maintained by a managed socialist economy. This was in contrast to the Steppes well location in a vast wilderness of grassland, flowers and bird life. We arrived in Rostov at our agent's office or, as John preferred, at 'Naughty Nina's Place'. Between Anya, Vita and Nina it was hard to give a winning title on John's view, as all three were showing their beauty plenty: minimally attired as was their fashion throughout the Volga region that spring.

The arranged meeting with Constantine, both the local Volgotanker representative and the person to know that particular day as it was his birthday, proved an extremely soaking affair, both in the river as well as out, from the vodka. We were all welcomed to join his personal vintage river cruiser styled on the WWII MTB torpedo boats for a two-day birthday bash. At one moment, I spied through the mist one of our BEST fleet steaming gently past as we howled and waved from our cruiser. The day's birthday revelries gave his office crew notice and time to prepare for my departure, which was solely dependent on when Constantine was ready to stop drinking and finish my immigration paperwork. Sometime over the following days, I joined the crew, like supercargo arriving on deck with a mobile herbaceous border given the quantity of flowers I had collected for my inaugural trip from Rostov through to Kerch, across the Azov Sea.

It became abundantly clear from my pigeon hole cabin that Volgotanker do not spend money on internal decoration or comforts. I had a starboard porthole, joined the shared common drop loo and shower and, when not in my cabin, spent most of the three days lurking amongst the eight mix crew that congregated on the lower poop deck. There was no alcohol on board, or none on offer, which was a delight as the constant stream of OhYha fish soup was potent enough.

On the third morning, following a lot of sleep, thought and reading, the port and starboard land horizons appeared to accelerate on a converging course to where, on radar, flashed a long streak that could itself soon be made out in the form of a pontoon bridge joining the point of Kerch in Crimea to its proximal equivalent relief, off the coast of Krasnodar. In a short time, the spot revealed the Tsakos owned 145,000-ton tanker – *Kriti Sea*. From our open bridge, I could make out the tiny dark face of Sharif, amongst numerous others, leaning and smiling with compulsive joy to welcome me into his creation, and what a wonderful sight it was to behold. The sheer size of the vessel compared to ours translated from elation into fear as I climbed a rope ladder up the side of this mighty tanker.

We toured our mothership, waved farewell to my Volgoneft 135 and then politely disembarked by jolly boat back to harbour and onwards, by car, to Sevastopol, for a quick historical tour, and then Simferopol to catch a flight to Kiev. Crimea held me captivated through my short drive of the historical places: Inkermann, Balaclava, Yalta and Kerch, only to mention the few that are joined by road along the moonscape-sculptured karstic limestone cliffs that front the Kryms Ki Hori topography into the Black Sea.

Permission to come aboard

1. *'Oligarch: n. A member of an oligarchy.*
2. *'Oligarchy: n. A form of government in which all power is vested in a few persons.*

I have considered the use of the word oligarch, that occurs only once in my narrative, and realise I should perhaps expand on the recent changes in its connotation. My narrative commences in the early period of the Yeltsin presidency and concludes coincident with the last months of Putin's second four-year term in office; the latter a period dominated by the activities of those associated with the term, oligarch. The modern perception of this term, at the time of writing, conjures a series of images depicting publicised poisonings including those of Alexander Litvinenko, Sergei and Yulia Skripal, Dawn Sturgess and most recently, Alexei Navalny. The murder of Sergei Magnitsky in 2009 led to the introduction of international legislation, Magnitsky's Act, which provides government sanctions against foreign individuals who have committed human rights abuses amongst other criminal activities. The oligarchs that I make reference to in this book are not of this modern style, even if later their activities were to fall within the scope of the legislation.

My image is taken and developed around the reduced circumstances that prevailed across the former Soviet society at the time of my entrance there, in early 1993. The State and all state run industries were bankrupt, a major problem as these monolithic enterprises provided social welfare and liquidity throughout the Soviet empire. Volgotanker is a good case in point. This river sea shipping company was not just the largest registered owner and operator of maritime vessels in the world but an employer, child and adult educator, pension provider, allotment and food distributor and banker for hundreds of thousands, in addition to managing the capital assets of housing, shipyards and vessels. The company was responsible, directly and indirectly, for the wellbeing of the majority of the Samara and Astrakhan city population, to name but two of numerous other Volga River cities dependent on its social welfare activities. The extent of the company's influence and provision would reach into the Lena River and Omsk region of Siberia, and north along the Neva River directly to Leningrad.

This was the landscape that became fertile ground for the rise of the modern oligarch. State and oblast (county council) officials had no means or knowledge of funding, managing or raising private funds or procuring loans. They had neither the experience nor the access to acquire foreign capital. The circumstances at that time were not at all dissimilar to those that prevailed in western Europe, primarily France and Great Britain, following the Spanish war of Succession (1701–1714), which led directly to the introduction of a new economy including, but not limited to, paper notes as cash, convertible notes, share script and exchange providing liquidity. Mr Boris Berezovsky understood all this and presented a solution. He, along with numerous others (such as Richard Sobel, in the case of Volgotanker, assisted by Sumo and the Russian speaking Jocelyn Graham Wilson) undertook a program of acquiring from the locals their State endowed share certificates for nominal cash (which was most welcomed by the hungry locals and pensioners) and built up a majority ownership of the respective government industry. An unwritten agreement followed which allowed the State to relinquish all liabilities for those in the population that had relied on that State industry during the Soviet period. Upon receiving this exoneration, the State in turn gave the then privatised concerns an unchallenged monopoly.

Over the nine years of Yeltsin's term, these State industries became privatised, properly funded and modernised, which was extremely beneficial to the younger generation of well-tutored Russians that could maintain the pace. But it also brought corruption. The principle agent of the corruption was the power struggle and corrupt practices involved in achieving board control. It was that control that led to the title oligarch. The subsequent listing of such a company on a western stock exchange led to the real problems – power, greed and all that followed in their wake.

Chapter 16
Control in the Desert and Beyond

The lads had done a brilliant job in negotiating the relinquishment of Lasmo's participation in the Burun Production Sharing Agreement, getting a perfect result for us with money only changing hands on five distant and quantifiable gross production milestones in the future. The production milestones were attainable, if astonishingly high, in our view, yet we doubted whether we would ever reach the fourth and fifth instalments, both of which if achieved would be a dream and a pleasure to pay. (The fifth and final instalment payment was paid in 2005 to ENI owners of the Lasmo commercial rights following the acquisition of Lasmo in 2001).

In the meantime, we had three months to prepare for the handover on 1st August 2000 and, in a sincere gesture of cooperation and friendliness, Joe Derby, Lasmo CEO, kindly agreed to bear the partial cost and administrative burden to cancel whatever contract, contractor or parties not required prior to that date, at our option and choice. We immediately requested that he get rid of all foreign and local third-party subcontractor personnel except catering, all leased or rental foreign equipment except stores, leaving vehicles and inventory already paid and in country. This left only the foreign catering staff under contract. Without question, Mr Derby undertook his pledge and cleared the decks for the arrival of our administration that would centre on control of purchase and recruitment within the local community. All future civil engineering construction facilities, including all road, pad and service access construction, would utilise equipment purchased in Russia. Our oil field service equipment, heavy machinery and work-over rigs, coil tubing units and inventory was all acquired as new from China. On the appointed day, approximately eight foreign personnel, including myself, rattled around in our 100 plus man camp knowing that we held 100% of the foreign equity and control. I thought back to that moment seven years earlier, while walking through the Turkmen landscape of destruction and desolation, when I had realised 'control' was the objective. That same control which I confidently assumed would encourage foreign investors to invest if reassured of the export link. That link and hope would lead to having total control of the up, mid and downstream sectors of the PSA.

The reality then accomplished left just two outstanding risks, both of which still frustrated the city observer and financial analyst – cost and political risk. The former was again in our hands but the latter, in my opinion, would depend on whether we performed well on the former. I knew that the fiscal, royalty and crude production performance and return to date had not been financially beneficial or impressive for our host partner – Turkmeneft. The local television propaganda reported that the president, then in international favour and being dined by UK royalty, US diplomats and business leaders, was becoming less impressed with his only onshore foreign operated energy project. Sharif's more exact reporting told us that our project was very much in the critical eye of the pessimist local political lobby who, for their own financial benefit, unsurprisingly, would prefer their local operator to prevail.

By making the organisational and fiscal field changes in a public manner, we immediately gained local approval and goodwill. Our cunning attempt, like the broken light bulb seller in Ashgabat, to circumvent the president's obsession with internal control on domestic affairs in particular and prevent foreign assistance in health or social welfare projects was addressed through the opening of a dedicated employment recruitment office in Nebit Dag town, with an associated medical clinic that would provide immediate health checks for applicants.

All town folk were encouraged to apply, especially those with problems around pregnancy or tuberculosis conditions, the latter most prevalent in the community. It was not our intention to offer full employment to all, but rather that they have access to free treatment. This action, along with the informal fundraising for the only national orphanage, also based in Nebit Dag town, demonstrated our commitment to the region and allowed our star to rise amongst the local community, if not as far as Ashgabat itself.

The two-pronged technical program was basic petroleum field management. First, address the low levels of pressure support in the reservoir systems from many decades of exploitation. We knew we had to immediately apply artificial lift. Our program – simple, cost effective and hugely productive – was led in the field by Bertie Campbell, a natural leader who instilled confidence and inspiration in the local employees. His team implemented a program that took the gas produced and largely vented from existing wells, flowed it through a grid of surface pipelines to 60 old, sluggish or non-producing wells to be then re-injected down the outer annulus of the casing or supporting pipe. The gas would be released into the central producing pipe at a depth between 1500–2500 meters, start to rise naturally, and, due to reducing pressures, the gas bubbles would then expand and lift the weighty oil column.

The reduction in weight over the oil column, or downward pressure, would allow an increase in the oil drainage from the surrounding reservoir. The net result of this dynamic energised flow to the wellhead was greater accumulation and capture of additional oil from each well that would then be measured in the surface collection tanks. The net commercial effect was an incremental production figure of an extra 350–750 BOPD per well. The additional amount per well, over time and cumulative across the 60 plus well inventory, when hooked up to the reinjection system, was to raise our gross production significantly.

The second arm to our technical program would involve the drilling of new wells; this was led by a hybrid Native American Indian called Bryce, who had no formal education other than his adopted oil field knowledge and experience. Bryce would sleep under his work-over rig and talk pigeon Russian and Turkmen. A real oil field lad who, on one occasion around the campfire, felt obliged to let us all know his true feelings and admiration for Anya, visiting from Volgograd, when he blurted, "I would eat the peanuts out of her shit just to get that close to her ass."

We had, over our non-operating time, identified in the shallowest of the four producing sections of the Burun Field petroleum system, a geological petroleum play concept which had hitherto fallen on deaf ears. A brilliant geophysical and geological interpretation identified a paleo shallow river dendritic system or channels of oil filled sand that extended throughout the greater part of our licence area. The new concept was proven by a drilling program using our new work-over trucks. These cheaper Chinese units would drill in designated well locations, test and complete a well within days or a week, maximum. Each well would follow a similar pattern of flush production in excess of 600 BOPD, before reducing after a period of a month to maintain a daily production of 250–450 per day and cumulatively produce up to one million barrels over a 4–5-year life. In most all cases, the well 'pay-back' time was less than a month's net production.

Collectively, the technical program introduced by the Burren Petroleum Turkmenistan (BPT) team over the first six-month period as sole operator would continue to grow production, become more efficient and, by the seventh month and throughout our seven-year tenure, swing the fiscal balance of the PSA into cash positive. The president showed his pleasure by reducing the tax terms for the PSA from 25 to 20% income tax in the third year of our operator status.

In London, the financial markets were still flat on their backs from the Dot Com crash, which cast a long shadow from the tall sign that read – No IPO market for the foreseeable future. The rational investors in my fold – BVCP, Pictet, Baupost, Chios, Sunfloat and Balor – were content with our elevated operating status and foreseeable free cash generation from both BEST and, soon, BPT. However, the gallery, including Michael and Simon, Capital International and AIG, were less rational, being, as they were, fuelled by general impatience and personal intrigue. They were, and not without good reason, looking for an exit for their investment, or at least a new man with a white collar and tie to run this novice's valuable show.

Away from the Caspian, the African program in the Kouakuala license had also proved successful. Maurel & Prom had fulfilled their 'farm-in' terms by re-entering and placing on production both of the ELF drilled wells with a healthy cumulative 4000 bopd production that was being trucked to the refinery on the coast at Pointe-Noire. They had completed a 300km 2D seismic survey using a Chinese contractor on the exploration area that lay due north-north west. A third appraisal well had been dry.

The next expenditure, following the seismic processing and interpretation of the geophysical data, would be an exploration well. The cost of this well was yet to be appraised, but would be borne proportionally by all three partners. Andy showed his stern view in stoic fashion, unlike his trading partner, Pierre, who still believed the upstream exercise an interruption to their trading lifestyle. I introduced my idea of a merger of Tacoma Resources and Burren Energy Plc to the Burren board prior to the drilling of the Tacoma exploration well, but was turned down. Andy was not shaken; if anything he was more resolved to hold out until after the exploration well, which we estimated would be mid next year. This decision was not arrogance on behalf of the Burren board; it showed a distinct lack of risk appetite.

The corporate development and achievement that year had elevated my awareness of what success in the public domain does to the individual as well as the company image. I had consciously spent the past seven years being evasive and nonconformist with my peer group as a way of hiding the simplicity and weakness of my evolving Game Plan. However, the signposted IPO exit mechanism chatter amongst adventure capitalist shareholders, together with the political and operating exposure of a real business and tangible cash flow, would impact on our and my public image in a manner that I knew I would want to control, protect and respond to.

I drove a 12-year-old Nissan Pulsar (Sunny), enjoyed anonymity in seaman class seats and, on the rare occasion that I was found amongst my industry peers, came to revel in their long sideways stares of disapproval. I did not want to launch Diana or myself into 'business society'. However, I knew (for me alone) it must happen and I thought how best to prepare for that image change.

My mind reflected on the time Diana and I were returning slowly in our hired Ford Fairmount, devoid of hubcaps, from Baja California in the summer of '78. Easing our way along the Pacific Coast highway with one objective for me which was as yet not mentioned to her: to reach Carmel and a bar belonging to 'the man with no name', as highlighted by a similarly named TV program on the BBC back in 1974. Her instinct and patience broke after the 7-hour drive when my ignorance of our exact destination became apparent, and so it was a great relief when we found and entered an empty open-air bar enclosure that was the Hogs Breath Inn.

Rather out of character for Diana, she did not fully appreciate my frozen pillar-state until she noted the direction of my stare towards a tall chap and young girl, presumably his daughter, chatting in a business-like manner to the barman. For that brief moment, we were as an adult foursome set for a tableaux, but then they left leaving me still, silent and in shock. I thought of the incredible coincidence of being in the company of a man who meant so much to me and men of our generation – and was the purpose of our trip – from whose film work has come many a quotable line, including one that I took as meaningful in preparation for that public image 'A man's got to know his limitations'. This statement and a similar resonating tip many years later from Tony Craven Walker 'not to fall in love with your assets', would become my mantras to guide, control and lead my progress along that unknown path most successful business leaders must follow.

My Russian shareholders and their guests were perplexed, while attending a local pheasant shoot in the Winchester area on the 11th of November, when on

143

the strike of 11 o'clock, we stood down our guns and went into a solemn mood that lasted two minutes while pheasant flew over. The Turkmen ambassador mumbled, Sharif translated and Michael Pakenham moved to assist his Excellency into a position to fire which was followed by another mumble, translation and stand down from Michael as the bird was well past. There then followed another miss through the lack of attention of our guest, the twice honoured Hero of the Soviet Union and first man to walk in space, Alexei Arkhipovich Leonov, who at the time was engaged in discussion with Harry Trig, a near blind gentleman of greater age, just arrived on his mare. Alexei Arkhipovich was romantically taken by the arrival of the mare. As for Harry, he became engrossed in Leonov's cosmonaut watch from their first handshake. They were both soon in tears reminiscing the 1965 grainy black and white television footage of his spacewalk. Lunch soon followed with our hosts, David & Kate Buckett, as the day was made even more memorable as another of our Russian guests, who had opted not to shoot, declared in his toast that he was, after all, a pacifist. This came as a bit of a shock to most all, as we had been introduced to Vadim Bakatin that morning as the last Soviet Chairman of the KGB. That really did make our day.

Akhtar Sharif in front of one of the many producing wells

Chapter 17
A Great Loss

Shortly after the Russian Christmas break in late January 2001, we moved to our customary local Moscow hotel. John Stanton and I, along with any other Burren travelling folk when passing through Moscow, stayed at the Pallada Hotel which was located in a commuter district of Koncova. It was a cheap and sometimes cheerful place positioned logistically proximal to the centre of Moscow as Leytonstone would be from Piccadilly, with an atmosphere that reflected the national mood. A mood portending nationalism through a political renaissance bearing the return of popular pride manifested as xenophobia. I was into my eighth year travelling in the region and could converse politely yet meaninglessly in Russian with the local folk, order meals, chat about the weather and slightly more when in listening mode. However, I was never competent enough to persuade others of an opinion, save the declaratory language which more often than not accompanied a toast.

The Pallada Bar was my senate chamber where my skills excelled, but, on this occasion, I was finding the atmosphere and the reception hostile. The staff refused to understand me when ordering my meal and the neighbouring drunk took umbrage and insisted on placing his handgun open and clear to be seen on the table. I ordered a few vodkas which we drank together to stabilise the situation as I saw it, which left the drunk's state of offence in limbo.

A coincidence or a trend, the mood at the Pallada was reflected in a similar fashion by a change in approach from Volgotanker. Legalistic letters from a Moscow based legal firm started to arrive on a weekly basis at our London address. They were building a case, documenting a boardroom majoritarian offensive by BVCP which resulted, through collusion with the management, in our bareboat charter contract and BVCP's commercial gain. A gain made through the assignment of the charter to BEST as a third party. We had taken our own initial line of defence with our routine contacts and good office within Volgotanker, Samara. This approach had hit an official stonewall and was blanked by their personnel, many of whom were new or had recently been promoted when President Strokin and his old guard were removed. Our immediate interest was to defend our position but, in so doing, find out with whom we had to take up our case. Local enquires led us to the Moscow office of the law firm and a meeting with the newly appointed Director General of Volgotanker, Alexzander Alexzandrovic, and my first meeting with a 'New Russian'.

The image of the school playground bully best describes Alexzander. Like most bullies, he was not strong willed and chewed his fingernails indecisively. The unsightly moustache and slightly obese form only exaggerated by his suit two sizes too small, with greasy hair and a first-night actor's bravado, gave me the confidence to know that he was only an instrument of some higher power. Over the course of the meeting, I began to understand the changes that had overtaken our relationship with Volgotanker during the past six months: our largest shareholder, BVCP, had either lost or handed over control and influence on the Volgotanker board to a wholly owned affiliate of the Yukos Company, the largest privately owned Russian oil and gas company owned by Mr Khodorkovsky, a strong player with known political ambition and board control over Volgotanker. I was not particularly interested to know the purpose or objective of his action, knowing I would have been seen as merely incidental to his plans for global domination. My primary concern was to understand where we stood with respect to the forthcoming navigational season and our prospects of continuing the hugely successful transportation and trading business we had built up over the past two years.

It became obvious to both parties, yet more difficult for Alexzander over the course of the day as we both held our respective commercial and legal positions, that we were both victims of a dispute by proxy. It was clear that he had no legal basis to cease the term or reduce the value of our charter, as BEST had not breached the terms of the contract. Further, it was in Volgotanker's financial interest considering the dry dock expenditure due, to have BEST maintain and operate the 16 vessels under charter. With this clarity and my sense that I ought to respect his belief that an act of boardroom injustice may have been perpetrated by a 'majority', we concluded our meeting with a shared understanding: neither party present was the intended benefactor nor the delinquent, but rather the innocent agent from past events that did not involve BEST.

I knew that I had done enough to retain both our course and assets for the forthcoming commercial season. I was also aware that I was operating Russian assets in Russia with overt commercial value, which displayed an equally overt contractual weakness. A weakness that, over a period of time, would cause failure in competitive Russia. The outcome of the day's meeting presented a difficult path to follow over the time remaining: legal challenge to our Volgotanker charter party would destabilise my relationship with our largest shareholder, BVCP, and result in questions being asked regarding the future commercial benefits of BEST. The question, and need to arrive as a transparent IPO investment vehicle with an expansive and transparent transport and trading profile, was weighted against our wonderful star, BEST.

Within days of the meeting with Alexzander Alexzandrovic, I travelled with Andrey to Omsk in Western Siberia, ostensibly to view his crude separation and cleaning process using centrifugal systems. The Omsk refinery was massive by any international standard and capable of producing thousands of tonnes of raw waste material from the vast amounts of crude delivered at the refinery gate. The contemporary waste product was collected together with the sheer volumes of environmental filth remnant of both Soviet and more recent times for the 'cleaning' process that supported Andrey's contract to export, by rail, low-grade fuel oil or gasohol product to load ports on the Volga River.

The following day, I left Andrey sick with flu in bed and went out in the frozen wasteland tundra in western Siberia to join a deer hunting party. I was once again dressed in my Russian infantry Siberian kit, but this time with the addition of a woodland patterned camouflage with pressed woollen boots. I waded my way through the drift light soft snow in a blue sunny 20-degree day. A distant single-engine plane could be heard resounding around the horizon yet never beyond my hearing or into my eyeline which was confusing, until a herd of deer came into view chased by the plane on skids with no wings attached. This amazing sight of Siberian ingenuity and adaption completely took my interest in the hunting away, such that I was to blame for the party's initial failure to kill, a mantle kindly bestowed upon me by a real hunter down the line.

There followed a long period of total silence as the Siberian afternoon light bounced the coloured haloes off the frozen drifts of flying snowflakes and I fell into a gentle snooze while camouflaged against a small tree. Stirred by a wood break, I notice that a stag was only a barrel length from my position. Again, I couldn't do the deed as it was just all too perfect; after a moment, the stag moved off alerted by a neighbouring gun. After the butchering of the carcass and an open campfire meal of the liver, we headed for home over a rough trail in the army off-road vehicle provided. A large glass of vodka given to me was quickly followed by a long disdainful glare from the Siberian killer who had viewed my weakness in allowing the stag to escape. He proceeded to sink his large tumbler in one gulp and wait for me to follow likewise. This I couldn't do and instead took advantage of a rough moment of passage in the road to spill near most all before taking the last drops with teenage gusto. He was not amused.

Back in our single room digs without service, I too came down with the flu. Realising, as one can from the forehead heat the depth and despair that accompanies a bout of flu, I managed to open the fridge to retrieve a frozen item of open sliced meats before joint pain prevailed. My last action was placing the spread of frozen meat over my forehead prior to losing consciousness. The scream that woke me as she took stock of my face, melded with raw thawed meats, told me that I had survived the night and the ordeal, but my survival certainly didn't help with the housework as my butchered appearance had given such a shock to the cleaning lady we never saw her again.

Burren's new London office was the centre of our universe. The office area had been the Turkmen operations centre for Monument, then Lasmo, who kindly honoured and assigned the lease to us before surrendering to ENI in December 2001. They had managed to persuade the landlord to allow us, a mere private company of unknown value, to take over the lease. The open floor-plan with a central formal boardroom and galley kitchen area allowed the mix of the upstream white-collar team to take the former and the midstream scruffy sailors the latter and, for the fluorescent European dressed downstream folk, I had prepared the largest corner office. This transformed the space completely into a seductive hotel foyer layout to match the trader's secretive nature. The conditions were perfect for both seamless communication movement between the three operating theatres, confined under one roof. Burren was a unique player and operator amongst its peers.

The legal letters, each with the cautionary action stamp 'Without Prejudice' piled 10cm high on my desk in a relatively short period of time. Their language and contents was becoming a distraction, a cost and a concern as the direction of argument was clearly destined for a London arbitration hearing, for which we had prepared and engaged a defence team. I was not concerned for the immediate commercial operation at BEST, as we had cornered our market for the season, way ahead of expectation, which may have been the source of their anger. Behaving as a subsidiary of Yukos, Volgotanker's initial practical response was to attempt through local court actions in Samara and Moscow to arrest and delay vessels, which on each occasion we managed, through our equally resourceful team, to resolve or deflect. Their objective in an arbitration court in London, we were advised, would be to win their case through a process of libel action. Whether successful or not, that would cast unhelpful aspersions on our major shareholder and other individuals on our board at a time when our corporate momentum was gathering pace toward a full London board listing. The tribunal effect or worse – a negative judgment – could severely discount the NAV of the company due to the political risk and foreseeable legal implications such a result would have on BVCP board members and other associated parties.

The mood change I had experienced in Moscow had taken in Samara before flowing on down to the Saratov region. Report and personal communication from Alexey indicated that our crude was being 'stolen' or, in their words, 'redirected' to a tank farm operated by the regional competitor, Sidanco. What had been cheered as a technical and commercial success by the authorities and local operating community not 12 months past, was then seen by an influential and controlling major Russian player in the region as an example of intimidation and corruption of local officials by foreign parties which should be terminated. The style and manner of the circumstance that ultimately terminated our technical involvement was pure Capone, when Alexey was killed in a 'private' and unrelated incident resulting from a grenade explosion that was never linked to our commercial entanglement. I learnt many years later that Alexey's brother, a minister in local government, had been kidnapped and held to ransom by a local gang led by the corrupt chief of police. Against personal advice from Andrey, Alexey had been party to the process of making the ransom drop which had gone wrong.

This extremely sad event was appraised as a private affair which just happened to involve Alexey Bandorin, our key partner. With his loss, we had no local or regional traction as our oblast partner and operator was toothless under the circumstances and powerless to respond.

What is common to all rural Russian life, is the protection of their own future welfare and state pension through adherence to authority. This fate, however, did not seem to apply to Saphonos, the director general, with whom I made a feeble attempt to mediate using the capitalistic image of the wealth created and promise of future awards to be bestowed through share participation. My effort was cleanly shown the door when he asked me to match the $100,000.00 on offer. I understood his position, knowing that he had no conception of the value of shares regardless of the tenfold valuation figure promised.

With a lack of remorse which I felt went with the territory, I took the loss of both Alexey and the Saratov project on the corporate chin. We knew that the Joint Cooperation Agreement was based on operational trust and it was that trust which eventually gave way through a series of dramatic events. I was further pitched into evaluating our Russian exploits alongside our Turkmen and Caspian Sea activities in light of the board's intention to go public with a company listing. The commercial loss of the Saratov upstream venture would have no puncturing effect on the momentum or fiscal margin of Burren, as the exponential growth from Turkmenistan remained strong. However, my attempts to build a diverse portfolio were blown. I had taken on board from my flurries into the market more than a year earlier that we were a single strand fiscal operation. Our dependence on Turkmen goodwill was clearly evident. The lesson from both Russian activities, Saratov and BEST, could benefit us by reducing the political risk in my story and corporate presentation. I was shameful of my materialistic approach to what had been a disgraceful and costly human affair but eight years of living in my self-created bubble with a fisheye exaggerated view of greed in the investors, competitors, city analysts and employees, was numbing my core sensibility and fundamental purpose of giving it a go.

President Nicolai Strokin, Alexei Arkhipovich Leonov
and Akhtar Sharif

150

Chapter 18
Swings and Roundabouts

It was on a beautiful late summer day at my favourite Giovanni's Italian restaurant off Covent Garden that I received news of the exploratory well M'Boundi no 1. It was a success; a commercial cracker. Using Helmut's mobile, I immediately called to congratulate Andy and gather more detailed information. From a geological perspective, the well came in on prognosis, forecast and plan, encountering the fractured basement Chela formation. From a commercial viewpoint, the formation reservoir rock encountered had temperature and pressure levels that implied a strong producing reservoir in place, filled with a light, sweet crude oil. The chemistry of the crude was indicative of a lacustrine continental diagenetic petroleum system which supported a 'rift & drift' paleo-environment regional play and tectonics, best conceptually explained by the continental spread of Africa from South America.

Andy was in disbelief at the news, yet the reality of the success would soon prevail as we discussed the next and immediate steps in light of the imminent directive from the operator, Maurel & Prom, to commence drilling a step-out well. This was the obvious and appropriate action for a fully cashed up operator with political and commercial avenues of address. Action that would score highly in both the net asset value of Maurel & Prom being, as it was, listed on the Paris stock exchange and having Denis Sassou Nguesso, The Congo President, with whom Jean Francois Henna, the Maurel & Prom CEO and majority shareholder, had an excellent working relationship.

However, Tacoma Resources were neither those of a listed company nor flush with cash that could be immediately sunk down another hole. This predicament highlighted the game change that happens with a shift from short-term trade liability management over to long-term sovereign investment programs full of liabilities. The liability brought about by the well's success immediately overshadowed the obvious financial gain, as the need to support the accelerating work program and retain Tacoma's working interest became an urgent priority. My memories of the Burun PSA signing event, or those in my seismic contractor days when any long contract was awarded to me, were of a two-minute spell of conscious enjoyment before the hard reality of immediately having to focus on funding hit home. Tacoma, as a trading concern, was up against that rock and the massive wall.

Prior to our departure from Australia, I had taken my daughter Milly and my father on a day trip to Kalgoorlie, WA, to visit the town and explore its gold mines open to tourists which sat amongst others that were still operated in the old gold diggers' town. Deep down, in dark silence, we experienced the sense of the surrounding weight and the touch of the gold vein dimly lit by the old miner's torch. While my father's thoughts drifted to the lads that had left his part of Kerry in the 1920/30s to make their fortune in the gold fields, my thoughts tried to conjugate the sheer wealth that had been collected and generated over the years. Why was that wealth transferred to a foreign bank and country? Wealth that had gone through the town and district only to leave it barren, similar to the majority of the state of Western Australia? The answer lay with the investors and, as the investors neither lived nor worked in the region or the state, the wealth was exported. While I could accept the historical precedent for the early 20th century and foundation of the state of Western Australia from where my family and I were soon on course to leave, I took note of the changing tide with yet another resource cycle booming the WA economy: how the state had recently awarded a licence for the first casino in its capital town of Perth. I concluded that this new approach was the perfect West Australian State financial structure: a gold mine beside a casino.

With haste, following Andy's permission and supported by Atul and Brian, I took, for a second time, the proposal that Burren should acquire Tacoma Resources for private shares in Burren to the board and, this time, received a majority in support of the proposal. The minority, principally Michael and Simon, were not in favour on the personal grounds of their further dilution and of not wishing to advance my equity interest in the company further through the acquisition of my interest in Tacoma Resources. The commercial and investment knowledge of the private equity managers present, furnished with their appreciation of our current single thread business profile, whilst very successful in Turkmenistan, was still but a single thread. Here, before them all, was the offer of a wildcat well success with a strong technical supporting view to promote its project development and, thereby, become a second jewel in our crown. The board gave their approval for Atul to complete the business acquisition on terms that would take an initial minority holding through Burren and assume the costs of the next two wells. Thereafter, the remaining rights were to be evaluated on the two well program and result, which would then quantify the project development and projection. What had first occurred to me back in early 1995, as a joint interest, became a more valuable reality for Tacoma and a huge future value for all Burren shareholders.

The weekly legal letters continued to build on my desk as did the volumes of traded and transported product from BEST transhipment operation. The navigational season was concluded with the *Kriti Sea* slipping her moorings fully laden and steaming for Singapore, her final discharge destination. Sadly for BEST, this was the final act of the most amazing single-handed commercial shipping venture transacted in the region since the Noble Brothers in the 19th century.

The dark clouds, not just from Yukos/Volgotanker but also Lukoil and related parties, were thick with contempt at BEST's profit and gain from their refined product. Through our transhipment operation and notwithstanding our ability to continue, I could see the obstruction that these major refiners would enforce to end, or at least financially impair, our transhipment operation. As a result and without a trading transhipment vessel option, BEST's future would be scaled back to the Caspian Sea alone. This course of action was the primary Game Plan course and our return could be seen as a benefit to our political standing in the region through alternative ventures with either Kazakhstan or Iran but not Azerbaijan, as an historic feud with (Soviet) Russia over the legal territorial offshore limits in the Caspian prevented Russian flagged vessels from entering Baku or neighbouring Azeri ports, or Caspar Azeri flagged ships entering Russian ports.

It would prove to be the case as, the winter having closed the river navigation season, John, Anya, Jennifer and I made frequent visits to Astana to meet with the political rising star of their evolving Kastransoil Group, Mr Kairat Krimmov. Following the most bizarre course of failed meetings, together we built the foundation of their shipping venture and national crude carrier, Kasmortransflot, the flag of which was a computer-generated collage created by John and Sharif.

The M'Boundi no.2 well proved to be a dry hole which caused immediate concern to the uninitiated, but was totally within the bounds of probability given both the poor seismic coverage and scant sub surface knowledge of the structure. However, it proved too much for Mr Buckingham at Heritage who took the well's commercial failure as his cue to exit, leaving with a $30 million cheque from Maurel & Prom (for their 30% of the project) or one million dollars per percentage point of equity sold. This figure gave valued assistance to the Tacoma deal and indeed expressed comfort for most all concerned, as the figure would prove to be insignificant to the final award, yet massive when considering the entry price of $300,000 that Tim Torrington had secured for his Heritage owner and company just over five years earlier.

Chapter 19
Just One Last Shot

The crude oil price had declined from what was seen as a dizzy height of $27 over 2001 to an average of $23.00 in 2002 and into 2003. Our emphasis since August 2000 on cost control was proving effective, as we continued to reduce the operational and capital cost per barrel produced down to single figures and toward the lower end of that spectrum, which was rewarding, as we grew the gross production curve from the Burun Field above 18,000bopd. On these figures, Burren would be considered a midsize oil and gas producing company if it were on the public market. However, the market for IPO listings in London remained subdued if not totally devoid of activity. My opportunity to make a Burren corporate presentation, inclusive of the 35% interest held in Brazzaville Congo and 100% Burun PSA interest with direct attention to the Paris listing valuation of Maurel & Prom made for interesting practice for what I knew would soon be the real thing.

Since the incorporation of Burren Energy Plc and, in particular, the arrival of Hywel, our administrative housekeeping had greatly improved, but none more so than the incentive scheme that became the matrix for a good team. I had taken stock of the moment when United Geophysical had been taken over and the majority female administrative staff, all of whom where long serving employees, enjoyed discussing their cruise choices and second home locations on the back of the sale. I had also noted the monthly news reports across corporate Australia in the early '80s of a corporate raider scam known as 'bottom of the harbour' fraud, where a takeover company would legally transfer the pension cash over to a new company, leaving the acquired company, present and past staff, with no pension funds. I had listened to Brian tell of the numerous share option awards that went straight into a loss on the basis of poor timing, poor management or both. With these tales and memories in mind plus the foresight to consider that we, a veritable small fish in the big pool, may one day ourselves be subject to a take-over, I requested the implementation of an approved award scheme that was tied to our annual profit performance as well as a long-term incentive scheme, both of which were to be calculated to reward ALL Burren Energy Plc employees. The Long Term Incentive scheme was based on all employees of Burren Energy Plc receiving an award sum taken from a pool, which was calculated on a percentage gain of the premium value made at the time of sale or title change of the company. I did not implement a pension policy due to my acknowledged concerns and my belief that such a scheme would not have been beneficial if we were to have a relatively short corporate existence.

The legal pile of papers from Volgotanker had, by the anniversary date, reached approximately 25cm high and was distinctly in favour of an arbitration court appearance in London, with our defence witness list looking increasingly doubtful as the tone and offence from the Volgotanker team was confidently embracing the libel theme. The details relating to BEST, its role and cause were of no interest to either side's legal argument. My knowledge of libel cases was limited to the public statement of Andrew Neil when defending himself and the Sunday Times image: the best estimate of odds in a libel case was 50:50. This was simply not good enough despite the optimism from our legal team. In my view, members from our board's very appearance in a London court was enough to damage both its internal integrity and the reputation of our largest shareholder. The odds on chance of losing the case and the resulting local and Russian press publicity did not bear thinking about. All this extraneous potential damage being, as it was, at the time of our expected IPO was simply not worth the gamble. My personal preference was to settle the dispute and suffer the inevitable consequences to BEST, this being a result that I had already factored into our corporate development forecast.

With all the heightened pressure and drama of a John Grisham novel, the court preparations were advancing, with final touches being put on opening statements which were to be presented before the London Court of Arbitration the following morning. In Moscow, twenty-four hours earlier, John and I had entered Alexzanderovic's and the Volgotanker boardroom to commence a meeting that quickly became confrontational and proved to be pointless, being no more than a recitation of their declared umbrage. The real purpose of our meeting was to conclude the proxy business disagreement between a Yukos view of Russian business and a BVCP view. Both, I thought, were guilty of foul and majoritarian power plays on defenceless share registers. Both would have been required to disclose this activity in a London court, yet only one would have to suffer the consequences of their action in the western media (my view would be demonstratively altered by Russian political history thereafter).

Maybe it was because I had been forced to address the publicity over the previous months or just that I desired a conclusion to this prolonged and distracting affair, but I made the first offer to settle. Wishing to take the advantage of our current up-to-date knowledge of dry dock cost per vessel in our fleet of 16, I nominated an even division of the bareboat vessels. My list of our retained vessels, identified by vessel name or number, would appropriately reduce the monthly charter fee and greatly reduce our dry dock cost for the foreseeable future. My nomination, of course, was inclusive of the *Astrakhan City* and *Samara City,* those being the most recent builds. They proceeded to play the bully, the kid with toys in the pram, the victims, the shamed locals and we the nasty foreigners, all of which we had to sit and snooze through until a settlement of exactly that which had been proposed earlier, with the exception of the *Samara City,* was accepted. Our settlement proposal went to draft and got signed off by 5am the following morning, exactly seven hours GMT before the London tribunal opening statements. That clear, clean early spring morning, as we walked along the Moscow streets to find an open metro to take us back to the war rooms at the Pallada, revived my enthusiasm for this Game. Just as a nervous passenger relaxes once lifted above the turbulence into the clear air, up onto a better and safer future, I rode the metro back.

Without BEST's transhipment programme, Burren's operational and corporate profile was simple: a diverse geographic upstream company with operational assets that could mitigate the associated political risk. The mitigating assets being the remaining fleet dedicated to the Caspian, and interestingly, Tacoma's trading relationships and history of intervention in the Brazzaville Congo. Both were off balance sheet and therefore not considered material to a potential investor's due diligence, other than comfort.

The investor story had fallen into place, with an actual and potential growth in the core asset value of our proven and probable reserves in both Turkmenistan and the Congo. Corporate growth funded with the free cash and working capital generation from Turkmenistan, which would be invested into low risk/high reward exploration and development in the Congo (following the dry well there was a sequence of over 40 successful commercial wells drilled over the following five-year period). Our corporate state was as close as I could get it to making a reality of my soft sell on Burren as the company with the West Australian economic and structural equivalence of a gold mine beside a casino.

With most all the risk taken out of the Game Plan and the momentum rapidly gaining toward an IPO timescale in the near future, the gallery boys had one last attempt to lance their boils with a show of solidarity and, for the first time, this included the support of Mike and BVCP. The institutional shareholders had taken a view, or as I saw it, they had got far enough into their MBA business manuals to be impressed by the perfect picture image of a white shirt and tie CEO with neat trim hair to know that there was a future that they wanted for Burren.

I was taken by surprise as they marched into our offices along with someone with that exact image, who I knew from an early Turkmen oil and gas conference, requesting I join them in the trader's corner office. This ex-Amoco petroleum executive had usurped the founding CEO of Nations Energy, managed to ruin the emerging company over a three-year period and was seeking fresh prey. The same man was attempting to cuckoo his way into Burren following an impressively long lunch with my gullible MBA kids.

The timing could not be better to benefit and reward his credentials through share schemes and more, as the company was taking the leap into the public domain. I remained silent unless spoken to. It was amazing to experience the situation and watch as each timed their commentary and support to remonstrate how wonderful my actions had been but that the future of Burren was all about the city, and in my hands... I waited for the turn of Mike hoping that his common sense would prevail and be the deciding voice. His turn came. As if coming out of a stupor after an adrenaline shot to the heart, he had a Damascene reversion and recognised that it was me in front of him. After a short time, he got up and walked out quickly followed by the rest of the thieving crowd. I never heard further and went back to my team.

Soon thereafter, and possibly in subliminal reaction to their attempted coup, I hired an experienced investment banker who had lost his directional instinct in the maze but could, in my view, be extremely useful in navigating the administration, compliance and the big Yellow Bookish world of the listing process, which would leave Hywel to concentrate on housekeeping and money making. Andrew Rose was the last to join our inner core team and he fitted in well. I took note that although I was the only non-Oxbridge member of the Burren executive I was not the only band player, as Andrew also played in a band. Oddly, this small patch of common ground gave some comfort to my sense of my own limited academic credentials.

Andrew's immediate effect was to deflect and terminate the endless representation and presentation material constantly arriving at mine or the front desk. These advisory teams were alert to our direction and in much need of a fee mandate as their market in these last two years had been poor. The process took a course through a number of beauty parades, somewhere we had our best frocks on and others where we tasted their claret. As in any natural marine feeding frenzy, the odd shark did arrive to taste the appetiser which, in the case of Addax, the emergent new upstream venture company, came with an unacceptable purchase offer of $100million. This offer was a pleasure to receive, not least because one of the broker firms invited had given us a value not higher than $50million and suggested that we should list at a price of $30million. The IPO market being subdued, there was no interest from any of the large or international investment banking firms, including Barings, and after a natural cull our choice came down to Momentum or Seymour Pierce. Both were small investment brokerages with limited experience in our sector, but Seymour had my old acquaintance from the early days – Mr Richard Redmayne. I was not compelled to vote for them because of that connection as I was initially unconvinced by his Etonian manner, which I saw as a hindrance to our mutual ability to present together – his background and style being, as it was, the antithesis of my own. However, the thuggish approach of the former manager tipped the scale and got my vote carried by the rather lovable manner in which Richard claimed that he knew people with 'more money than God'. For something quickly becoming an event that was Richard's to win or lose, or so I naively thought, there were a few amongst our shareholders that were betting on the latter.

On the eve of the roadshow and the run onto the public listing process, I was confident in my salesmanship abilities that had been honed from my experiences in Australia, but I was far less sanguine about my public speaking skills.

Belief in your ability to tell a story well comes from knowing that you have played a founding part in the formation of all its detail as well as overcome the many pitfalls that came with constructing its narrative, whether it be a piece of equipment, a building or an operation. It is these sorts of stories for which you alone have sole royalty in the telling.

For Burren, I was the best candidate to tell our story, not only because I was the founder and CEO, but because I wanted it to be heard with the modest style and decorum faithful to those early days when anonymity and bravery prevailed. I knew that the whole unvarnished truth of my adventure was out of the question for the somewhat refined ears of the professional investor but, I was told, the unbending confidence that comes with telling your own story brought with it a bravado the city boys and girls would savour and come to embrace.

I should have expected the bravado and 'supreme' confidence infused from the informal congratulatory receptions would hamper my style. Yet despite those introductions and the applause for a game well played, I did not express a clear sense of a mountaineering success. On route by taxi to the first all party meeting, including TSB, the lawyers, Ernst & Young accountants, a pair from a financial public relations firm and the Seymour Pierce team in their office off Poultry Street, I sat there comfortably anxious and took stock of the moment. The direction of travel was once again into an unknown territory and, for me, most unlike all previous experiences, as I came to discover that it took the form of a gentleman's club.

Andrey Pannikov, myself, Charles Clancy, Akhtar Sharif
and Michael Calvey

Chapter 20
Into the Jungle and Beyond

Three years of formal, unqualified, audited full year accounts permitted us to apply to list on the full board of the London Stock Exchange. That, together with the expectation and inducement of a dividend announcement, propelled us through much of the Yellow Book administrative requirements. I was completely out of my depth on most aspects of the procedure, including but not limited to the requirement of financial public representation, internal and external broker analyst coverage, buy & sell brokers, share underwriting and so much more that, on a bad day, there would be one that exploited my weakness and another that dismissed most all as the duty of others with a higher pay grade. The market over the year had only had four IPOs past the line, a record from which one could interpret that numerous others had been pulled. Moreover, the window of opportunity was narrowing as we moved into autumn, with a decisive limitation drawn of mid-December or the Christmas office party as the official closing date.

There remained one important housekeeping act to fulfil that involved a non-executive shareholder director to sign off. The Long Term Incentive scheme required, in the event of a change of ownership that a listing on a public exchange would trip, the company to firm a valuation prior to that event such that the gain or loss would be apparent as an amount to pool for an award, or not, for the eligible employee group. The board appointed an institutional shareholder and director, Stewart Gibson from the Capital International group to debate and anoint a figure. I was, of course, aware that this member of the board had been mostly negative about Burren and the IPO listing process throughout his tenure, as well as being instrumental in the attempt to oust me having, for some reason, found me to be a disappointment. Conversely, I thought that Stewart's approach and aptitude for money management was premier amongst his peers on the board. Nonetheless, he held a personal dislike for me. Regardless, we had to engage with his pessimistic view of the outcome of our IPO, something which was evident in the nominated share price that he agreed: $0.82. This figure would stand at the lower end of the spread up to the listing price, which I hoped and believed would be materially higher. The investor book would be built and a final price to list, compiled with Richard's consent, on the date of listing (on the assumption that was right) a percentage of that spread would be the amount shared between a small number of Burren employees.

The detailed comprehensive listing particulars book had been prepared and printed with every page highlighted with the quote, 'This is a high-risk investment opportunity' once if not twice. A future three-year forecast capital expenditure program for the company claimed centre stage and served as the pinnacle to the £2 million cost of production, as not only did the figures have to compute but the implications had to be approved and signed off by our auditing firm, Ernst & Young. A book presentation, in slide form, plus maps of the Caspian and Southern Russian, and the West African coastline central to the Congo River constituted my working material. At each and every port of call in the forthcoming road show, the attendees would be left a copy of both the Listing particulars and my presentation material.

Following two unofficial dinners with Richard's clients that proved unsuccessful, the Richard-Andrew-Fin show officially moved and camped in Edinburgh, with a solitary unsuccessful trip to Glasgow to present to Gordon Bennett. It was the first Edinburgh meeting, in casual surroundings and a sandwich lunch, where we picked up our first genuine or soft circle level of interest from the Artemis manager and long exponent of the political risk inherent in small oil investment. Standard Life and Scottish Widows both held their favour for Scottish based North Sea players. Both joined the Burren shareholder register a few years later. As I had earlier hoped, I found real joy in telling my story and watching the listener reach or move from genuine interest to stultified amazement upon hearing my dreamer's fairytale of lands they had neither heard of nor would ever expect to take their children, as I had taken two of my daughters, Tessa and Sophie, the previous summer. It was my belief that their fear of political risk would ultimately control their corporate purse strings. I got good at reading the situation within minutes from their first look at my maps: whether to take the expansive route or the short cut to the next meeting.

In London, the show got into its stride with six or seven daily sessions plus a lunch presentation back at the Seymour Pierce office. This, over the weeks, made one certainly feel for the patience and persistence required of actors on a long run show, especially on matinee plus evening performance days. Andrew disappeared, for family reasons, for the majority of the second week which allowed Richard, previously the understudy, to rise to the occasion. Andrew's departure was not before I caused a stir while presenting to Investec. Tony Alves, their analyst, was distracted by the lack of a sugar bowl. I had thought it most odd, Andrew using both hands in an eastern manner to drink the coffee I had poured.

There were further humorous moments when I made one complete and successful sale with the Caspian map presented upside-down throughout. Another with the energetic arrival of a youthful fund manager with cavalier confidence and an announcement that he already had an investment in the Congo, "Which Congo?" I equally energetically replied.

"Are there two?" he retorted. I knew that I had lost that sale.

We beat our way around the city investment funds and shops with a daily business lunch interval, taking only one day out of seventeen to go for a shoot in Kent, which led to the selection of a prescribable date to list – 7th December. Not once did Richard drop his chiselled city good looks to offer me any encouragement as to how we were filling the book, other than a foot shuffle or grimace, the kind that your piano teacher would give you after getting three lines of sheet music correct. Perhaps he just didn't know.

There was little or no fanfare as we approached the list date, as most all considered the market moribund, with only the interest of Christmas at the end of a poor financial year to offer cheer. I had arranged for Andrey, who had never contemplated going to Africa but felt that he should being as he was a major shareholder, to join me at Heathrow on the evening of 6th December to fly together to the field and well site in the Congo Brazzaville via Johannesburg. I ordered a number of cases of good champagne to be delivered to the offices of both Burren and Seymour Pierce and left the country in relief – relief born as much out of gratitude that the arduous showboating had finally come to an end as fear of being present for a dead cat bounce share entrance the next day.

At 7am on 7 December 2003, ten years and ten months since I entered the Intourist departure lounge at Domodedovo airport, the Game Plan was officially given a market value of £175 million, accumulated through the listing of 134,615,385 shares on the full board of the London Stock Exchange at a price of £1.30 each. Tessa, then reading economics at Nottingham, called home later in the day to asked what was going on as she had received three marriage proposals that morning. I cannot be certain as I was on the M'Boundi oil field with Andrey throughout the day, but I believe the cat did shuffle as the share price dropped over the first day of trading, by one penny. Thereafter, it never once fell below the listing price.

Before that first day of trading, I had transferred ownership from my own shareholding, 36,000 fully paid shares, to Roisin, Charles, Vicki, Bertie and Jocelyn equally, with a further 300,000 shares to Adrian. This group consisted of those that had contributed to, but were not able to participate in, the Burren share scheme either by their own choice or ineligibility.

Over the following four years, one month and 25 days of Burren Energy being a publicly listed company, most all of the value and interest of the company, and in me, was documented and is held in the public domain. The company, with no long-term debt, was sold for cash at a share valuation of £12.30 on 1st February 2008, valuing the company at £1.74 billion following events that commenced with an unsolicited phone call.

****

Addressing the rite of passage, the confirmation of a public listing amongst the hydrocarbon sector on the London Stock Exchange led to the reckless risk-reward standard act of choosing to take on greater risk. Risk that in the private sector would necessarily not have been considered as good business sense. One of our first acts as a public listed company was to sign, through Brian's good work, two exploration licences in Egypt and, later, one in the Republic of Yemen. These debatable acts were countered over time when Atul engaged with his Indian compatriots to acquire a 37% minority interest in the Hindustan Oil and Gas Company. Both proved to be exciting, as we participated in drilling an offshore development gas well in proximity to Chennai, in addition to two unsuccessful wells in the Egyptian desert.

The Indian prospect, although readied for production, had no contract to sell the gas. Primarily due to local political foul play, production was temporarily suspended. Our 48 million cubic feet of daily gas flow was eventually hooked up on a secure commercial contract to the offending electric power generating station, an event which took place in part through our support of the political opposition who won the next state election standing on an egalitarian manifesto that included a mandate to supply black and white television sets to all low caste families for free. Their communities would in due course require a cheap electricity supply!

Our expectation was to take a majority shareholding in the Indian company, but, like Saratov, our technical success proved to be our own corporate downfall, as a politically powerful shareholder, Mr Deepak Parekh of the HDFC corporation, refused to sell on hearing of the accomplishment despite signing over to us the legal rights to acquire his equity.

I enjoyed being a shareholder and director of an Indian concern, especially one that held interests in the Gujarat region where I had spent the late summer of 1988 boarding alone in a destitute rural shed with Guja, a rat that gnawed through my cheap leather valise on a nightly basis to acquire the seismic data for the National Indian oil company, ONGC. Much like I had lost out to the rat throughout the survey time, we found that our commercial experience in India, in particular the deception and corruption, was more onerous than Russia.

The Burren work-and-play ethos was never more pronounced than in 2002 and each early December thereafter up to 2007, when we took vacant possession of blighted semi derelict or 'haunted' houses somewhere in the British Isles. At one of the latter locations, a scene making a mockery of wit provided the humour when a temporary member of the accounts staff enthused us that she was a medium, but soon left the party after Adrian Skelt caustically mentioned from behind his newspaper that she was, in fact, a large.

Commencing in the Burren, the London office staff and foreign operations guests, without spouse or partners, would gather for a long weekend filled with all the required food and beverage by the vanguard team led by Sharif and Kamila Fullbrook. Each year would build on the last to fuse the unity and confidence of the team through the fun and farce that was brought on amongst the general hilarities of the secret Santa where the clear divisions were shown at a £5 limit present. My present went down a treat with Hannah, only for my standard to be spliced as her name was Rebecca. Or the annual awards: the last being won by the CFO, Andrew, for the least valued item to be claimed on his expense account – a light bulb.

By the third year as a listed company, I was peaking in my promotional style, supported, as was to be expected, by the extreme fortune of a bellowing wind of ever-increasing crude price to assist our success in building our net crude oil production to in excess of 30,000 bopd from both geographic hemispheres of operation.

The power and success of Burren in the public domain was testing my philosophical principles. The combined tensions which came with a love of my new assets and an ever-present knowledge of my limitations stirred airs of arrogance or worse, hubris, which I found difficult to deflect. I was extremely conscious of our success and tried to maintained my travel style of tube, bus and seaman class flights at all times when travelling alone although my actions did, at times, have consequences: the bus was superior to the tube for local connectivity and would permit telephone conversations at as quiet-a-level as possible. On one occasion whilst on a telephone call on the No.9 bus to Kensington, I discussed my recent meeting with President Niyasov of Turkmenistan. Notable key words, together with the international business flavour and general topic of my conversation, brought the attention of my fellow travellers such that when I moved to get off at my stop the lady beside me commented, 'that was the most interesting bus ride conversation I have heard for years'. On another occasion, fellow passengers on the upper deck of the No. 11 began to observe with interest as I detailed over the phone our impending tender for an exploration block in Kurdistan and the alterations to our business proposals. A commute home provided the 'Bridge of Spies' moment on the crowded train back to Winchester. The look of awe on the lad with the *Evening Standard,* comparing my mugshot in the business section with the man sat in front of him cramped into the window seat of the carriage. I did not wish, and thought it better not, to change habits or cars but Richard Redmayne had convinced the Board that my 18-year-old Nissan Sunny was a death trap. Emotionally, I drove the vehicle to a breakers yard and, with a sense of accomplishment akin to a Himalayan climber, went off and bought the first Ferrari I saw in its place. However, as no insurance company would accept the circumstances of a man whose previous car history peaked at a Nissan, it remained in the garage and I continued on public transport.

His Excellency Saparmurat Turkmenbasy (Niyazov) meeting with Burren Energy

I was bereft at the death of both Roland and Andy so soon after we went public. With Roland, I had managed to sneak down to his country estate, without his family's permission who was trying to hide his state of health, a week before we floated and just three weeks before his demise, to pay my deepest and most sincere respects. Roland was the man I considered as my corporate patriarch. Andy's passing was more sudden and a massive shock. He left his family lunch table, while on a well-deserved early New Year holiday, to have an afternoon nap and simply never woke up.

The loss of Roland and Andy was felt by many, as the former gave everything in reputational support and encouragement whilst the latter provided access into the grimy chamber of power along the West African coastline.

Reflecting on it all I held firmly to the belief that Burren Energy, possibly along with many other young companies from diverse sectors, owes all of its success to the principles and actions undertaken while a private concern. That private, entrepreneurial time was a period when dirty hands and sweaty moments were embraced with a creativity and determination which, on entering the public domain, seemed to dissolve overnight into clean and manicured gestures of publicity motivated management decisions that reported on everything yet motivated nothing. I realised that the public listed corporate manager, whilst the same person, was destined to be humoured and favoured, or possibly not, by the financial analyst, broker, advisor, institutional and private shareholder and financial press like a child in a fairground. The manager's only purpose was to prosper if only to meet their exulted expectations. The recent past world of real business and political risk was off limits. That was until, against board approval, I slipped across the Turkish Kurdistan border in a taxi one summer night in 2004 to accompany a group of Russian oil service men to the next possible business opportunity. The event, while invigorating, sadly proved not to be profitable as we were either too early, introduced to the wrong players or both. Either way, three years passed before we made some headway in that geographic sector, only then to be cut short by corporate events.

I knew, by 2006, that my limitations had been reached over the past thirteen years promoting the organic business growth of the company. I reflected on my natural inability and lack of desire to embrace loan capital or print new shares in order to exchange them for other company shares. The personal result of this failure was, in effect, to maroon the inorganic growth of the company. I knew that I was not the white collared MBA boy that the Gallery shareholders wanted a few years earlier. I was also not the marauding raider out to ravage the city world through mergers and acquisitions. A world that, on the whole, financial history records as a world full of lost shareholder value.

Shortly after announcing our annual results in the April '06, that year, the share price broke through and was in excess of £10. By my own philosophical marker, I had reached my limitations. With the comfort and knowledge that this next corporate deed was an act which I had conceived of and predicted more than twelve years earlier at the first formal management meeting with Monument in 1994, in that April 2006 I asked Atul to take the role of CEO of Burren Energy Plc. He embraced my offer as the chess player taking over from the poker player.

Late in February 2007, Atul and I were being driven along the Bombay corniche when I answered a call on my mobile from ENI. I was rather confused and lost by the Italian's belief that we were committed to selling our interest in the Brazzaville Congo. Our sale, as he understood it, being part of the confirmed sale of Maurel & Prom's interest. This was news to me and only seemed to further confuse and amaze my Italian caller. He understood, from Jean Francois Henin, the CEO of M & P, that we were accepting their deal back-to-back. I gently repeated my earlier comment and then added to his bewilderment that we would retain our rights to exercise our pre-empt clause over the deal following a detailed review of the ENI's offer to Maurel & Prom.

There then followed a month-long period of political table bashing by the world's 6th largest oil company, utilising all their political and street credentials along the West African coast to force President Denis to demand our sale.

I took the opportunity and swept off to China to meet up with my man at CITIC, the China International Trust Investment Corporation. This septuagenarian chain smoking kingmaker, shortly after Burren went public in 2003, sat me demonstratively lower down and told me to "go out there, find the oil as we in China can't and when you do, come back and sell it to us".

With Mr CITIC's blessing, an overnight flight and a few days later via a day trip to the president's jungle retreat, I made it back to Southampton. The UK immigration asked where I had been for such a short time following such a suspicious itinerary: 'A quick lunch with the Congolese President', I replied and walked through. Against the odds, we had managed to secure a pre-emption of a further 9% points of the Congo project to bring our total participation interest up to 40%. We were delighted with our success, as the price paid by both ENI and Burren valued the project in excess of $30million per percentage point.

That summer day in Sochi had not gone to plan and especially not the way our politically astute Russian partner had proposed. The expense of our chartered flight and hotel, just to sit in the adjoining meeting room to where Putin was making a private visit to the southern Russia business development seminar, seemed unnecessary. The purpose of the trip had never received my endorsement, but then politically motivated and aspirational people will always support such action. Our conceptual sour gas project proposals for the mighty gas fields of Astrakhan had been reviewed locally as well as by Gazprom in Moscow with some acknowledgement and interest, but by no means their full support. I could accept that a political hand from Putin would have been beneficial, but my scepticism that we would get the chance opportunity or time to garner his attention on such a detailed subject proved correct. I noted a missed call from ENI as we left the auditorium, which I duly dismissed and assumed was a wrong number.

Why it is that big business ideas have to be shared at early morning breakfast meetings in five-star hotels which, for me anyway, only ever generate a dry-cleaning bill to dash my enjoyment of a rare hot breakfast, I will never know. It was extremely difficult to enjoy my Savoy Full English under the watchful eye and constant interjections of my ENI hosts who were constantly declaring their rational business sense and desire to make an offer for my company. What they were expecting me to do or say still remains a mystery to me, other than the only thing that I did say at the breakfast: 'If that's what you wish to do then don't let me stop you'. Within a week, or, more specifically on 9th October 2007 (Diana's birthday), ENI made an unsolicited cash offer at £10.50 per share for Burren Energy Plc over a RNS announcement to the London Stock Exchange.

How we must have annoyed them with our Congo manoeuvre. On that price-per-share, I computed that we stood to clear a massive profit on that Congo pre-emption deal alone. Atul, our CEO and corporate chess player, went into bunker mode to defend our position and introduced, within a month of the ENI offer, a White Knight in the form of the Korean National Oil Corporation, who made an offer of £11.50 per share. Rather than identify with individual original shareholders, Atul performed confidence tricks and miracles on the board, to get a board vote of rejection for the offers. The board's refusal to sell was upheld formally throughout the official offer period and, with no further improvement on the price from either party, the official offer was rejected and the official acquisition time elapsed.

David Jamison, a VITOIL founder and trader of note, travelled as my guest that year to join Andrey and his team of duck killers to spend the week on a house boat moored along one of the many banks of the Volga River delta. We had made this event an annual trip over the past six years to entertain guests and dignitaries which included Mike, Kalinin and Leonov from BVCP and, on two special occasions, had Richard Redmayne along with his box of Bloody Mary ingredients, particularity Clamato juice and garlic salt to spice the local vodka.

Throughout the offer period, I had kept my own counsel. That particular November morning, standing in silence in my punt, musket in hand looking out southward to the end of the earth that was the Caspian Sea horizon, I concluded that we must sell. The philosophical dogmas had bounced and thrashed around my mind like a pinball throughout the offer period. Was it the ping on the sensors declaring my love for the assets and awareness of my limitations, or was it pure timing? Was it recalling our first equity oil value from the Burun PSA in 1998 at approximately $20 per barrel versus a 2007 average of $74? I returned for the morning break to confront Andrey with my firm view that we should sell. He agreed, as did Mike and Kalinin of BVCP, who also spoke for and knew the views of Pictet, Beaupost and AIG. Without hesitation, I immediately got

170

through on a poor line to Mr Scaroni, CEO of ENI, who just happened that day to be with Mr Putin. How cosy we all were, me on the Volga and him in the Kremlin. Mr Scaroni was pleased to hear from me as he wanted to get a deal done – a deal which could then move forward on a private basis. He also insisted on the last word "Finian, you may be a great oil finder but you are a poor business man". I did not defend myself, wedded as I was to the business principle that when a deal is done, or near done, then the less said the better. I, along with my major shareholder, took the view that only time would tell whether or not this would be a correct decision. However, and in the meantime, if I could get the price over £12.00 per share then I just may have a chance of getting that view.

By the end of the month, the negotiations were revived with new vigour. Although the intention to complete a deal was known by a limited few, each one of us felt the force of that wish. Over this prime negotiating time, my movements were limited to remote hill drives along the Scottish border lowland country, with my guests enjoying the thrill of missing extremely high partridge. Between drives at the partridge, I would attempt, through poor signal, to maintain contact with the negotiations. I was told later by a member of the Burren team that my cool attitude and patience to the price movement kept the ENI team on edge and compelled them to up the price, as my silence was taken as a rejection. What was not understood by both teams was that I was, for most of that crucial time, out of signal on a hill drive and, as such, could not and did not appreciate the situation.

The agreed and final price of £12.30 per share was confirmed by me over the phone following the last drive of the day. Later that evening in the Black Bull pub in Laudar, I participated in a landline telephone conference board meeting to confirm the price and sale of the company. The deal was to headline the Companies section and featured as the leading news item on the next morning's *Financial Times* newspaper.

Eventually Paulo Scaroni and I did meet at a pre-Christmas lunch. In a private room and with his time short, we enjoyed no.11, 34, 56 & 73 from the Chinese menu at China Tang in the Dorchester. Following his departure and with a bill in hand for £187.50 but a minimum spend requirement for the private room of £1000, I selected a 1990 bottle of Lynch & Bages for a very private Christmas party of Atul, the attending waiter and myself. The all-cash deal closed on 1st February 2008 (my birthday and the anniversary date of both the Burun PSA Effective date 1997 and the Bare Boat Charter 1999) for £1,740,000,000 as the daily spot price per barrel of Brent crude rose through the $90.00 barrier. Atul had the final job of distributing amongst the 22 London staff the resulting incentive pool of £25,000,000 with the closing words, "we have changed a lot of people's lives".

Hywel John, Brian Thurley, Akhtar Sharif, myself, Andrew Rose, Helmut Mayrhofer and Atul Gupta having a good lunch at Giovanni, February 2020

A tale of unlikely success; of one man's journey in oil exploration across four continents before climbing the foothills of the London Stock Exchange.

An often times lonely voyage of ambition and irrational perseverance, where knowing who you're not is just as important as knowing who you are.

"That particular November morning, standing in silence in my punt, musket in hand looking out southward to the end of the earth that was the Caspian Sea horizon, I concluded that we must sell."